The Ayahuasca
Guidebook
and Journal

The Ayahuasca Guidebook and Journal

Discover Ceremonial Healing
and Transform your Body
Mind and Spirit

Hannah Milward

Published by Tipi Press,
an imprint of Lasavia Publishing Ltd.
Auckland, New Zealand
www.lasaviapublishing.com

ISBN: 978-1-991083-29-6

Contents

Acknowledgements

I'd like to thank my mother, Shirley Milward. Thank you for carrying me and birthing me into this magical world. For unconditional love and acceptance, for selfless generosity, for the long hard hours of work, for teaching me acceptance, compassion, and grace. I'd like to thank my father, Phil Milward. Thank you for being a pillar in my life, for showing me the balanced masculine, the gentle, kind and compassionate yet firm protector. For always having my back, no matter what, and for also showing me unconditional love and acceptance. I'd like to thank my brother, Dan Milward. Thank you for teaching me resilience, deep forgiveness and how to work with triggers, for being an example of transformation and courage, for teaching me how to dance like no one is looking. I'd like to thank my love, Joshua. Thank you for showing up in my world, for your passionate love and acceptance, for the adventures, the support, the soft quiet moments. Thank you for pushing me to grow, to become all that I can be, for supporting me so beautifully, to feel my fears and move through them anyway, for always aiming to leave people feeling better, after they experience an interaction with you, for dancing with me, like we are the music. Thank you for your work, for helping so many people on this planet. I'd like to thank my tribe in New Zealand, you know who you are. Thank you for the love, support, friendship, the vulnerable, intimate connections, the walks in nature and deep conversations.

My Letter to You

Hello, beautiful human, thank you for investing in this work. My name is Hannah Milward. Of course I am not defined by my name (or the things I have done, or continue to do), but perhaps the words that follow in this letter of introduction, will give you a feel for what I'm about and why I felt called to write this book.

I have spent over fifteen years working within the 'healing arts,' for want of a better descriptor. I am a trained Nurse with a background in bodywork, movement therapy, exercise science, integrative hypnotherapy, trauma work, and other healing modalities. I have also always been interested in nature's healing gifts, with a belief that the best medicines are un-refined and we 'just need to know where to look'.

I have a broad experience with various plant medicines, from herbal teas and homeopathic remedies, to using psilocybin, san pedro and of course, many experiences with ayahuasca. Working with plant medicines, meditation, art, movement, breath work and nutrition have been integral parts of my personal healing journey, a journey that deepens and continues as more 'layers of the onion' are peeled away. The work never ends.

Plant medicines found me after many years of being very curious and holding an intention to one day have at least one experience. I first sat in ceremony with ayahuasca two weeks after a psychic saw this beautiful medicine in my field. This life changing opportunity came to me. I did not have to seek it out.

Since that first ceremony, I have journeyed regularly. I gave up counting, but in 2023 alone, I attended twenty-five ceremonies and did a lot of travel. Twenty-five ceremonies is not a huge number for those who facilitate, but it is certainly enough to have gained useful understandings worth imparting to others.

When I began to work with these medicines, I had no idea how my life would be transformed by these plant spirits, and the humans that work with them. Little did I know that the medicine would bring me to a place where I would be travelling to South and Central America, helping out in ceremonies, and offering support to participants dealing with the difficult experiences that can arise. After almost giving up on intimacy following some relationship traumas, and coming to a place of peace in my own space, I would never have imagined that this medicine work would lead me into a positive relationship with a medicine man.

When I discuss plant medicine in this book, I'm predominantly talking about ayahuasca. When I refer to other plant medicines I call them by their name. The ceremonies discussed in this book are generally carried out in group settings within a retreat environment. There are, however, many ways of working with ayahuasca, and much depends on the lineage of the shaman conducting the ceremony. These days, you can choose a pretty luxurious setting with a modernized approach. You can also choose to go traditional, deep into the jungle.

The ceremonies discussed in this book are carried out in countries where this medicine is legal, (Peru, Costa Rica, Brazil, Ecuador). There are also regions in the USA and Europe where ayahuasca is decriminalized, and most parts of the world have some allowances for ayahuasca use when it is associated with the Santo Daime Church.

Why this book? Why now? Many of us are seeing the need for change and seeking out plant medicines. These medicines can, for many, fast track the processes of awakening and creation. However, it's not uncommon to feel somewhat lost after our first experiences with these powerful plants. And this feeling of being lost or stuck is not limited to plant medicine retreats. We can feel this, 'okay, but now what' after yoga retreats, meditation retreats, self development courses etc. and can experience a sense of sadness, anxiety and groundlessness in the days and weeks that follow the initial afterglow we receive from fresh inspiration, insights and explosions of self awareness. Words will never do justice to the work we do with plant medicines. Nevertheless I will do my best to share insights, stories and ideas, to, hopefully, help others along this path.

Before my first experience with ayahuasca, I had many questions, fears, and hesitation. I was physically prepared, but I did not know what to expect emotionally. I did not know how to take my initial insights into my daily life, how to process what came up for me, or how to keep doing 'the work'. This book aims to help readers avoid the struggles that I faced. I would sometimes come crashing back into old triggers, patterns, people and routines, which fragmented the clarity previously gained. It would feel almost as if there is no path to walk forward upon, a sense of groundlessness.

I needed to keep doing the work, keep the inspirations alive, keep living the change. But how and what to actually do? This book acknowledges that the honeymoon phase after any transformational or inspiring life event can wear off fast. We all need tools, prompts and a path of self-inquiry to keep our goals and aspirations alive. To truly move forward on our paths, we can't walk alone.

I believe that in order to create with full force, we must clear a path, clean our wounds and process traumas that limit our beliefs. As our beliefs shift and change, the world around us follows suit. When we move from fear into love and trust, we find ourselves living in a more loving and trustworthy world.

I talk to many people who sense an inner purpose wanting to surface, an itch within that needs to be scratched, a calling inside that wants to be heard. In approaching this, people seem to have an awareness that our personal baggage needs to be unloaded. We can't get clear on our true purpose, clouded by fear and doubt. Others argue that we must learn to be brave, take responsibility and let go of a reliance on systems that no longer serve us. With clarity, we can create from a place of fearlessness, freedom, compassion, and love.

This book can help you prepare yourself, your loved ones and your environment for the transformation you will experience when working with plant medicines. I mostly discuss Ayahuasca, including important 'fundamentals', the how, what and why, the benefits and the risks. However, the book may also be useful for work with psilocybin, wachuma (also known as the san pedro cactus), therapeutic ketamine, MDMA, etc. This work aims to assist you in 'finding ground' after leaving a plant medicine retreat, or other transformational experience.

The book is divided into three main parts: preparing for your transformation, what to expect during your work, and how to keep working after your initial experience. I have written with the intention to help maximize the potential for long-term growth, and positive outcomes for those of us venturing into other realms for healing and transformation.

Within these pages you will find contemplations around self-awareness, a familiarization with emotions, and the ways in which we gain self-awareness by tuning into the body. I will present thoughts around specific topics and self-reflection questions, to assist in the unpacking of your transformational experiences, your past, and where you want to direct your life in the future.

I will also discuss processing your deep experiences with art, breath work, and movement exercises. I include recipes that will make your pre/post ceremony diet a little easier and more enjoyable, perhaps even inspiring you to get creative and improve your nutrition outside of 'ceremony time.' Please bear in mind that any advice should be adapted according to the guidelines you have received from your own retreat or ceremony organisers.

Dispersed throughout the book is a little about my personal experiences, my life, as well as insights from others regarding their own healing journeys. While reading this book you will be invited to look within, to get curious about your history, your triggers and find ways to grow your inner tool kit. Throughout, I will present ideas around ways in which you can keep transforming yourself and through that, the world around you in meaningful ways.

Finally, a disclaimer, this book is not a replacement for personal counselling, or medical support. If possible, I encourage you to work personally with a healer, guide, holistic or somatic therapist, especially if you are struggling with what might surface while working with plant medicines.

I hope that you find this book enjoyable, useful, fun, and constructively challenging.

With sincere love and gratitude.

Hannah Milward

Part One:

Preparing for
Transformation

Personal Reflections

My first experience embarking upon a plant medicine journey was deep, profound and life changing. I saw relationships from entirely new angles, and from the perspectives of others. I came out of the experience with a 'love and compassion upgrade,' I was more sensitive and vulnerable, overflowing with insights and ways in which I wanted to change.

However, I made some mistakes in my preparations. I did not allow for any time to 'decompress' or process the experience. I had to return to work and 'life stress' immediately following my experience. I struggled to express what changes I had gone through, and rather than just 'living' the changes, I became frustrated at the general lack of words to describe all that I had been through. I did not expect to struggle so much with speaking my new truths and changing routines when faced with old triggers. Setting new boundaries around what I wanted to consume (cutting back on toxic food, entertainment and company) was initially a huge challenge.

I now make sure I prepare. I express to those close to me that I will need space and to expect some changes upon my return. I take some time off work and I ensure I don't succumb to peer pressure if invited to engage in entertainment that doesn't align. True friends and family will love and respect me even more when I stand in my truth, speak up and set boundaries. I have dropped the need to explain my experiences. I now do my best to embody and live the changes (using the tools that you will see in the pages that follow).

Preparing your Nest

Imagine, your partner, sibling, parent, child or best friend going away for a week or two and returning to you, as a totally different person. We tend to get uncomfortable, to say the least, when those closest to us suddenly and dramatically change. Change in others can bring up our own triggers, deeply challenge us, and destabilise our own patterns. Before you venture into a plant medicine retreat, it is wise to 'prepare your nest.' By this I mean preparing the space in which you expect to return, following your retreat or ceremony.

Remove Toxins

It is important to remove toxins from your environment. Not only what foods and drinks you consume, but what you watch, listen to, who you spend time with and the environments you choose to enter. Before embarking on something like a plant medicine ceremony or retreat, it is wise to take a look at what is serving you and what is not.

Set Intentions

It is wise to set some intentions before diving into the ceremony space. Powerful plant medicines warrant our respect. They are certainly not there for our amusement. One should not spontaneously decide to go to a ceremony on a whim, rather, we should muster up the courage and venture into this space with clarity, conviction, and intention.

Preparation - Writing Prompts
Getting clear and
Setting a Foundation of Self Awareness

- WHO in your community do you know that seems to bring you a sense of wellbeing, positivity and harmony? Who are you with when you notice your body relax, a feeling of flow, like you can say anything - and feel safe? Maybe the 'who' includes pets and animals out in nature?

- WHAT are you doing when you sense inner peace, a relaxed alertness and general wellbeing? Maybe yoga, dance, walking in nature, doing art, playing music, cooking, writing, reading... the list is as long as we are different!

- WHERE are you when you feel most at peace? Walking around museums, out in nature, laying on a beach, climbing a mountain, a special space in your own home or garden, at community gatherings, a theatre show...

- When you return from your transformational experience, who will you be living with?
- How can you prepare the people you live with so that they can support and accept a 'new you'?
- Jot down some initial thoughts and ideas.

_____

_____

_____

_____

_____

_____

_____

- Who will you be working with?
- Can you ensure that those you work with can be accepting of any changes you come back with?
- List out some things you may want to say or express to those you work with that may allow for a more harmonious return to work.

_____

_____

_____

_____

_____

_____

- Do you need to prepare your peers and social group? You might need to express that you may change your habits and routines.
- Can you think of a few things you might want to say or express before you leave, to prepare them for a new you when you return?

_____

_____

_____

_____

_____

_____

_____

_____

- What will you be consuming when you get home?
- Do you need to have some supplies ready for your return that support dietary improvements?
- Consider listing some key items you wish to remove, and items you want to stock up on for your return?
- What kinds of entertainment will you engage with upon your return?
- Consider looking up some ideas around positive creative endeavours you can plan to engage in. Are there classes, workshops or high vibe music or events you wish to attend?

_____

_____

_____

_____

_____

_____

_____

_____

_____

_____

_____

_____

_____

_____

_____

_____

_____

_____

_____

_____

_____

_____

_____

_____

_____

_____

_____

Self-Awareness 101

Being our 'best selves' requires us to be in the driver's seat of our lives. Gaining self-awareness is a key that can help us to unlock insights, important insights that can open us up, help us to develop better presence, active engagement, and empowerment in our lives.

With self-awareness we can choose to act, rather than react. We can set boundaries and take responsibility. Knowing ourselves means that we can consciously lead ourselves, and others, through life's challenges and constant changes. Awareness is a foundation and pillar for personal growth, wellbeing, and the wellbeing of those around us. Getting to know and understand ourselves is a huge task and can feel confronting. It takes a willingness to be vulnerable, to see and feel our own darkness, and our shadows. It requires courage, bravery, and honesty.

If we look within with sincere honesty, seeking to understand our deep unconscious and the many layers that make us who we are, we can quickly see why inner work is important yet often avoided. Sometimes we avoid it until we hit rock bottom. Getting real with ourselves can get somewhat uncomfortable, as we often see some aspects of our inner landscape that challenges the 'ideal' identity we wish to embody, and the way we want others to see us. Of course, it's much more comfortable to remain blind, and to wear a mask.

Many of us, walking this path, seeking to go deeper within, have experienced some kind of trauma. We might have a recurring issue in our lives, or carry a disturbing personal behaviour we want to change. We are generally not looking to take plant medicines for recreation. Many of us have suffered due to the actions of others. Sometimes those who were supposed to care for us caused us great harm. If this is you,

you are not alone. Most of us who have experienced trauma, have told our stories countless times, hoping that talking with a therapist will help us leave the past in the past. Finding an experienced integrative or holistic therapist who can skilfully hold space and truly listen without judgement, is a powerful step towards healing, and why I recommend working with a healer or therapist of some kind.

Sharing our stories in a supportive space is important. Crying, feeling emotions fully, and releasing what needs to be released with words, is healing to a point. But there is that point where re-vivifying our negative experience no longer serves us – unless of course we get desired attention or special treatment, which can be an unconscious yet understandable and perfectly legitimate desire. When we tell these old stories repeatedly, with the same emotion that we felt at the time that the event (or events) occurred, we bring them to life in the brain – over and over again. The brain re-experiences these moments, as if they are happening here and now, and we carve out deeper and deeper neural pathways around our story.

Luckily, we can heal. It is never too late to move towards empowerment. We can change the impact and nature of memories with simple practices that I will go into later in this book. It can be uncomfortable seeking help from humans, especially if we carry an imprint or unconscious story that humans are not safe to seek help from. Turning to plant medicines for help requires an immense level of trust. It demands courage, faith in the unknown (or unknowable), confidence in ourselves and our abilities, and a genuine willingness to embrace change.

Travelling to other realms to see ourselves with more clarity can shake us to the core. Sometimes the clarity we seek (and find) can be so shocking, disturbing, and even terrifying, that all we want is to run back into the shadows of ignorance. We are conditioned to run away from discomfort – and run fast. Yet this state of avoidance and running is no way to truly live. Our inner treasures are more often than not, hiding just beyond the pain, just behind the fear, the fear that can feel insurmountable but when we pass through it, we often find it was only ever about one inch thick.

Emotional and Sensory Intelligence

So many of us grew up in an environment where we were taught to hide emotions; that emotions were somehow weaknesses or an aspect of our being that we should be ashamed of. It is, therefore, no wonder we suppress emotions, or pretend they don't exist. Being mindful of our emotions and intentionally experiencing them—especially the uncomfortable ones—requires a warrior's spirit, along with immense strength and courage. Choosing to feel, rather than distract or avoid is the opposite of weakness.

Dense and uncomfortable emotional states can be highly challenging, but like everything that rises, these states must also subside in time. Although emotions are so much more than words, we can use words to help us meaningfully communicate our emotional state – and ride the waves that emotions form. However, we can sometimes experience emotional states, where the words that can paint a picture of the experience just don't seem to exist. That's also okay. Most of us can recall a feeling so big, or so difficult, that words escape us.

It may be that we need to sit with emotional states for a while to find the words, and to avoid projecting blame onto others as though 'they' are responsible for our inner experience. The important part is learning to feel and understand, while being gentle with ourselves and maintaining self-compassion. To grow and evolve, it's important to be able to identify and experience emotions (sometimes expressed outwardly, sometimes inwardly). Sensing emotion involves the interpretation of signals from internal and external stimuli. The heart, gut, intuition, skin, eyes, ears, mouth, and our thoughts. The perceptions and meaning we ascribe to stimuli have an impact on our feelings and emotions.

Our emotions can seem like the audience in the theatre, responding to the movie or show (the thoughts and content) that keep rolling through our minds. Being aware of the experience of the emotions, can invite us to pay attention to the content of the 'production' we are watching. If the audience (our emotional state) is panicking, what show are we watching? Is the movie or show real or imagined? Would the experience of the audience change if the content of the movie was consciously shifted? The answer is generally yes. The often unconscious content we play repeatedly to ourselves, impacts our emotions. Our emotions, impact our physiology and biology in milliseconds. The chemicals we release when in fear, stress, or anxiety change the chemistry of our blood, our cells and potentially the expression of our genes and DNA. For those interested in learning more about this, I recommend reading Bruce Lipton's 2005 book, The Biology of Belief.

Our perceptions of memories, our moment-to-moment thoughts, the films we play in our minds, our beliefs and our expectations shape our emotions from one moment to the next. This happens when we are consciously aware of it, and when we are not. What we call our 'emotions,' our energy in motion, is shaped by many factors: the underlying state of our nervous system, what the unconscious mind is tapping into and processing, what lies beyond our 'normal' perceptions, the movement of the planetary bodies in space, etc. The reactions and meaning we give to all the perceived emotions, shape our moment-to-moment reality.

Despite some people suppressing their emotions, they are always present. Some of us have been deeply hurt, we can almost forget how to feel – but when we allow ourselves time and space – we can 'reconnect with our emotions'. Our perceptions, interpretations and reactions can determine what kinds of chemicals are released into our bodies and how we then further respond to the sensations that these chemicals create. Chemicals, such as dopamine and serotonin, or cortisol and adrenaline (our inner pharmacy), are a key component of the well-known placebo effect and can foster either harmony, or disease (dis-ease).

In an age where most of us are running on the familiar emotional fuel of stress hormones, awareness is essential if we wish to drive our lives in any direction with intention. When we remember how to rediscover our ability to connect with our emotions, accept them, sit with them, process them and contemplate what the emotional messages are all about. All emotions (even the hard ones) can become powerful tools of self-development.

Emotions that rise within us and feel uncomfortable in the body, sometimes spark the 'thinking mind' to immediately grasp at a story to explain the discomfort. Some of us are living in negative environments or regularly experiencing negative situations, but we all have resources we can access. We must be careful to critique the value of playing on repeat, the negative stories that cross our minds. This may justify or enable old patterns, emotions, and ways of thinking to run our present state of being.

If this feels familiar, ask yourself: is this the story I want to keep active in my life? Is this really the movie I want to keep watching on repeat? With conscious effort and work, it is possible to experience the emotion, and refrain from giving it power by feeding it with the mind.

Taking the Mind to the Gym

Beneath the countless unique situations and surface-level concerns that bring people to therapy, a common thread often emerges—uncertainty and the struggle for control. Effective therapy helps individuals build trust in themselves, empowering them to navigate life's inevitable uncertainties.

Working on our minds is training and generally involves daily work. Remember, baby steps create change. We all have our stories, our traumas, our pain to bear and our journey to walk. Us humans, standing upon our current place on the evolutionary ladder, seem to need the experience of some darkness to know the light.

When we feel like it's all too much, we might do well to remember, every flower was once a seed that needed the dark underworld to grow. At our best, when we are living outside of 'fear mode', we are in-trust. We are always growing, accepting new challenges and opportunities that probably should scare us just a little bit. When we surrender to the magic of being alive and appreciate our capacity of being able to feel such a wide range of 'emotional notes', we can cling a little less to the 'good emotions' and be okay with experiencing the discomfort of the 'bad or difficult emotions'. This conscious appreciation of the lower notes tends to decrease our overall suffering. When we accept what unfolds around us—most of which is beyond our control, we often find a deeper sense of peace within ourselves.

When we dig beneath the myriad of unique situations and presenting issues, just below the surface of many problems is the concept of 'uncertainty' or lack of control. The purpose of effective therapies, generally involves equipping people with enough trust in themselves to handle the inevitable uncertainty of life, to perhaps even realise that possibility can only really live alongside uncertainty and possibilities beyond our wildest dreams present themselves, when we surrender and let go of control. We need to be able to find safety and connection within.

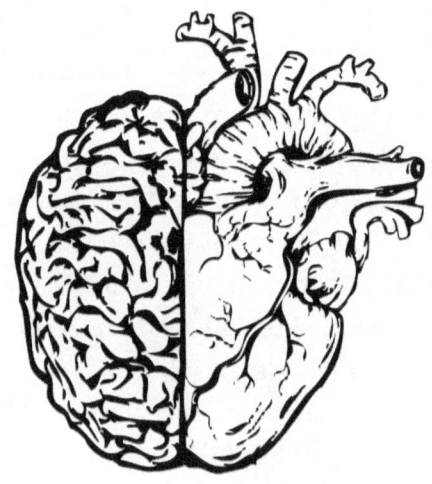

Ask yourself: What do you notice in your body (feelings or sensations), and mind (thoughts), that let you know emotions are coming to the surface?

Our emotions act like an inner navigation system — sensed as experiences in the body — and the body doesn't lie. The nervous system and intuition have a clarity and scope that the conscious 'thinking mind' doesn't come close to. The thinking mind often 'lies' about the present moment by tending to showcase the archive of the past. Leaving very little room to create a new action, leading towards a new reality.

Most of us react - based on a remembered past. This reactive pattern, then re-creates an outcome similar to that which we have recollected, and we say to ourselves: 'I knew that would happen, I was right', without understanding that our inner state, focus and strong 'imagining' has helped to create that which we potentially did not want to manifest in our lives.

The thinking mind can unconsciously attach to the status quo, even if our current situation makes us feel miserable or even creates dis-ease. Even if we find ourselves in a toxic or destructive situation or environment, the mind will often tell us: 'better the devil you know,' or 'at least you know what to expect,' or 'change is too risky,' or 'at least you have security in the current situation.' We all know someone who constantly complains of the 'dead-end job' or that stagnant relationship. Talking about leaving is one thing; acting is another. It can seem too big, too overwhelming. If only we were trained to be still, to shut our eyes, and ask our inner knowing: 'how do I want to feel instead, and what are the next smallest steps I can take that will move me towards feeling better?'

Change can be terrifying for the mind. Even the thought of 'losing control' can create stress. But can we actually become 'addicted' to stress? Kind of. By activating our nervous systems, and creating a cascade of cortisol, adrenaline and dopamine, stressors can also wake up the neural circuits underlying 'wanting and craving' — just like some addictive substances do. A stress-addicted brain might unconsciously seek out numbness through distractions to avoid dealing with the source of unhappiness or a loss of control. Of course, it's easier to be incredibly busy than to face any painful emotions accumulated during the course of our lifetimes

A stress-addicted brain, and it's accomplice — the body and persona, might unconsciously drive the need to spend a lot of time focusing on just how busy and stressful life is. Someone might prioritise adding more tasks to the list, say yes to more commitments even though they are already too busy for family time. They may prioritize piling on more tasks, saying yes to additional commitments despite an already overwhelming schedule. As work hours increase and free time disappears, social interactions and enjoyable hobbies are often abandoned in favor of chasing even more stress. Meanwhile, relationships slowly fade into the background. People who may be hooked on their inner stress cocktails, don't tend to feel happy. Their perceived attempts to move towards happiness or peace always seem to eventually involve piling on more pressure, expectations and stress.

A stress addiction will often stem from growing up in a household where stress levels were high at all times. As an adult, stress could be the 'comfortable,' natural state, the norm — even if it's miserable. The more stress we're used to growing up, the harder it is to have less.

The brain will also 'orient our focus' towards danger for our own survival. This was adaptive because we had to constantly be aware of the tiger in the jungle. Nowadays, this focus towards what we don't want can vibrationally match us with that which we fear the most. We may feel a 'connection' or feel drawn to a person, place or situation that ends up harming us. We may even unconsciously use this experience as inner proof that we can't change and life will always be painful, hard (insert negative belief here).

Change is work. It is our personal responsibility. Digging deep every day, to orient our inner focus, using the power of imagination, visualisation, and meditation — to sense, feel and concentrate on what we do want to become, seeing and feeling the full picture of our desired new identity and rehearsing that, rather than the old stories, is a core part of change work. Many of us, unfortunately have to hit 'rock bottom,' experience a crisis, an accident or an illness before choosing change, myself included.

Listening with Our Bodies

Learning to listen *with, and to,* our bodies can help us change our lives for the better. Our body sensations can be so overwhelming that we can (unconsciously) dissociate from our bodies as a coping strategy. Especially when we have been through traumatic experiences.

Two people often live the 'same experience' externally but are impacted very differently emotionally and physiologically. Thus trauma is not really what happens to us. It could be considered as a subjective experience, what happens *inside of us* because of the perceptions, reactions, and meaning we assign to an event. Something comes into our worlds. It's not perceived as safe. It's deeply uncomfortable. We have no tools, safe people or place to express what has happened, no support to regain our sense of balance — that is when we are impacted by what we call trauma. Thus Trauma can be understood as a *perception* of a threat or danger, and the experience of not being able to do anything about it.

Many of us, especially those of us who have experienced trauma, have not sat and really felt what's going on with our bodies in many, many years. We live in our heads and forget we have hearts, guts and an entire nervous system sending us messages. More messages are being sent from our bodies to our brains, than our brains to our bodies. And yet we are trained to be 'in our heads' most of our lives. So now that we know all this, let's take a moment to feel. We can learn to renegotiate the body's response gently by sitting with the feelings of discomfort or fear, knowing that this time, we are not trapped, but have the tools; the uncomfortable sensations will pass.

When people talk about emotions they often talk about triggers. The fact that we have 'triggers' means that we are carrying ammunition and something inside is ready to explode. Avoiding triggers or getting angry when we feel triggered does not disarm the weapon. To move forward in our lives, we can learn to take more responsibility as we gain more awareness of our inner weaponry.

Just like a knot or trigger point in the physical body, we can gently hold an emotional trigger, ease it open and watch it dissipate. That trigger can gently dissipate as we say to ourselves; 'What is any thought, that's not this one.' When we learn to observe and breathe through discomfort, it tends to become less and less. We become less reactive, less likely to blame others and more empowered. We may drop the victim identity and become victorious.

As we learn to gently move ourselves away from blame, we can take baby steps towards empowerment, actively shaping our emotional response from the inside out. When we notice an uncomfortable emotion we should acknowledge it. By increasing our levels of self-awareness, we can begin to choose a thought that feels better.

Often our reactions in the moment of a traumatic event are repressed and we stay locked in a frozen or paralysed state, both physically, emotionally and on a nervous system level, without even being aware of what is going on. The state of freezing, often occurs when we can't fight (or flee) from that which is hurting, threatening, or frightening us. We get stuck when we can't reach out for help, because help is not there for us – or because calling for help feels unsafe. We can get stuck in a state of fight or flight too, which we can notice in people's postures and patterns. Most of us, if we were to think of everyone we know or have known, can conjure up a picture of someone constantly 'flighty', on the go, posture leaning forward, always ready to pounce, anxious and stressed. When we have a healthy and regulated nervous system, we sit in a state of restful alertness, with brief visits into flight, and maybe moments of shutdown. But we move back into neutral. This ideal seems pretty rare these days.

We very rarely allow our bodies or minds to go through the process we are biologically designed to complete. We have all seen animals "shake off" the freeze response caused by a threat. When animals experience a trauma, they will literally shake it off, or carry out some other physical release, like snort, lick, roll around etc, which helps the animal discharge the energy of the distressing event. Just think of the idiom, 'shaking like a leaf.' It's often used to describe a reaction to a frightening situation. This trembling and shaking, from the emotional part, or limbic brain, sends a signal that the danger has passed and that the fight-or-flight system can turn off. When we see animals shake after big frights, they are literally finishing the nervous system response, to release the energy, or *'trauma charge'* from the body. Some animals can die if they are unable to shake off the trauma, and humans seem to develop mental or physical illnesses.

Humans will also shake off trauma as a reaction, but for many the 'shake it off' response isn't available, socially acceptable or allowed; so the trauma can be held in the body. Issues arise when something prevents the nervous system from completing the natural energy discharge response; such as being held down, held against your will, or being immobilised (*even with medication from medical personal*). In these cases, the experience can become stored in the body.

Additionally, we often repress the grief of neglect or abandonment. We often repress our anger, aggression and natural survival responses when faced with physical threat. Much of this *holding back* is unconscious. This 'held back' energy still exists in the system and can sometimes come forward in potentially unsafe or inappropriate ways later in life. For example, when we say we are 'triggered' and find ourselves reacting in ways that don't fit, or serve our present situations. Learning to be aware of what feelings and sensations mean to us, is foundational when becoming more self-aware, and self-awareness is a key to meaningful personal growth and development.

With help, we can learn new ways. We can discharge unwanted energy and patterns in ways that are adaptive and life affirming, rather than chaotic. Learning to feel old 'stuff' with a new lens is a good practice. Discovering a wiser and clearer lens can be an amazing process. Plant medicines can fast track this journey. They can help us to learn to feel our old stuff with a new lens, in seemingly magical ways that go beyond words or typical scientific explanations.

Exercise Finding your 'Truth Spot'

We all know what 'truth' feels like and we all know that the imagination can conger up a real sensory experience, so let's have a quick play with this idea.

This is a fun way to remind ourselves that we can not only think our way towards truth but also, intuit and feel our way to truth.

1. Find a comfortable place to be still for a moment and close your eyes

2. Set an intention to sense the truth in all things and find your inner guidance

3. Focus. Release any expectation that you may be holding onto. Allow the present moment to unfold as it is, not how you want it to be. Accept the moment

4. Inhale, feeling your lungs expand fully. Exhale any stress, tension and charged emotions.

5. Be quiet, be still, becoming more aware of your body

6. Say (out loud, or to yourself) a statement that you know to be true. *For example: 'My name is Hannah' or: 'I love and respect nature.'*

7. Notice the exact sensations, or spots within your body, that

'light up' as you speak truth. Also noticing the *tone, or nature* of sensations that arise. People commonly feel warmth around the heart, tingling in the solar plexus etc.

8.   Next; Say (out loud, or to yourself) a statement that you know to be untrue. *For example: 'My name is Freddy Mercury,' or, something you know to be the opposite of something you value: 'I hate nature.'*

9.   Notice the exact sensations, or spots within your body, that 'light up' as you speak a lie. Also notice the *tone, or nature* of sensations that arise. People commonly feel a 'constriction' in the area of the heart, or even a total body sense of 'repulsion'. Everyone senses truth and 'untruth' in unique ways.

Allow your inner guidance system to communicate and practice picking up on truth/ 'untruth' in your daily life, it is a great way to sharpen your intuition and get into the body.

Exercise - Your Powerful Imagination

Imagine a time when you were in a place that you absolutely love. Shut your eyes and really place yourself there. Notice details if you can. Who are you with? What are you doing? Observe your posture and your breath. If you are 'seeing' in your mind's eye, are you seeing a scene like watching a movie? Are you seeing from the first, or third person? Are you seeing in colour, or grey scale? What are you hearing? What smells are present in the environment? How deep can you go? What emotions arise as you play this mental movie?

Now imagine a time when you experienced something that you have some tension around, a little regret or anxiety around. Do you see yourself 'in' it, or watching, is this scene in colour? What do you notice in the background of your imagined scene? What emotions come up when you 'play' this movie in your mind?

It can be interesting to observe how our brains 'code' data, just noticing that all thoughts we think are recalled in the five senses, we think in pictures, movies, inner voices and sounds, inner recalled touch, smells and tastes. What we recall from an event changes every time we recall it, and the quality of our recollection can shape how we feel, and how we act or react to future events that 'trigger' a memory.

Think back to a time when you heard something that triggered you. Hear that voice. Imagine you can hold a remote control and turn down the volume. Or turn it on fast-forward so it speaks in a chipmunk voice. Do you notice a difference in how you feel about that memory? What will happen when you think of that moment in the future? Maybe rather than triggering you, it might just make you laugh.

Bring your mind to an event that left a negative imprint as a child, nothing major but something you know still carries a little charge inside. Imagine that event that hurt you, shut your eyes, ask yourself, "what do I have now, as a wise adult, that if I had those traits as a child, the whole scene would have played out differently"? Maybe a strong voice, confidence, strength (etc). Perhaps you can imagine gifting that child a strong voice or confidence, maybe the means to run away or even fight? Take a moment to really feel those resources (for example, confidence) that you have as an adult now. What do you feel like now, when embodying those inner resources? Who are you as a person?

While tuning into how you feel when you have all these tools, imagine that you can now send all those traits and resources down to your visualised child self, then re-direct that inner movie, see that child self use the tools that you sent down. Watch the 'child self' succeed in that inner scene. Imagine 'floating' down as your adult self. Give your child self a hug. Then take the child-self back with you, into this present moment, fully integrated.

Your conscious mind may 'know' you are imagining, but the unconscious that controls reactions doesn't know the difference between an imagined, or real, past or future 'memory'. Rehearse your new movie, knowing that the powerful unconscious mind works in metaphor. It is nonlinear and shapes your responses to triggers well before your conscious mind even knows you have been triggered.

Every time you can stop a negative or uncomfortable feeling loop by remembering something that brings a change to that memory, carves out a new 'choice' for the brain. You are essentially adding a new word or sentence to the old document and pressing save. Next time it opens, you can experience the updated version.

Fear, Guilt and Shame

So, now we have had a bit of fun playing with a little 'self-awareness taster', we should talk about some serious stuff like the things that can get in the way of *tuning into* our personal truths and developing our abilities that navigate us fearlessly towards positive change.

An Unholy Trinity?

The three emotions, fear, shame, and guilt have immense power, arguably shaping every aspect of our worldview and how we create our lived experience. Before we get into creating change, and the work of looking at and processing our traumas, it can be useful to cast our minds over these powerful emotional states. Hopefully, through reflection, we can build more self-awareness and self-compassion.

Looking at Fear

Fear is a natural response to perceived threats or uncertainties, but when it becomes dominant, pervasive and overwhelming, it can (and will) hinder our personal growth, creativity, and ability to be present in the world.

Fear has its purpose; it can keep us safe. But, experiencing something shocking, hurtful or harmful in our formative years can set up life long phobias. Even seeing a caregiver terrified or breaking down can wire that same fear into the mind of a child. We can find ourselves unconsciously focused upon that which scares us the most, honing in on the experiences, environments or people that can do us harm. Being hyper aware of where risks exist, might have helped us 'in the wild' but our lives have changed since the days when we were hiding from tigers.

With our intense focus upon dangers and risks, it's little wonder that we keep manifesting the same painful experiences that we want to avoid. If we keep these metaphorical 'tigers' in our visual 'range' we can avoid a surprise attack. But if the 'tiger' is a toxic relationship, and our biggest fear is abandonment or abuse (fears established very early on), we need to heal and overcome these fears. We must learn to focus our powerful minds, and senses upon what we do want, not what we don't want to unfold in our lives.

When fear controls our lives, we are significantly limited in expressing our full potential, in pretty much all aspects of life. Fear can make us risk averse with a fear of failure, rejection, or criticism, leading us to avoid taking potentially beneficial risks that could lead to growth. Growth and expansion tend to involve stepping outside of the comfort zone and embracing uncertainty. So when fear prevents us from taking these risks, we miss out on opportunities.

Apart from making us 'stuck', fear can feed self-doubt and diminish self-confidence. When stuck in fear states, we may question our abilities and feel hesitation around the pursuit of our goals or projects, convinced they will fail or fall short. Thus fear can truly stifle our gifts, our creativity and innovation. When we are afraid of making mistakes or being judged, we may find ourselves sticking to the 'safe and conventional' – rather than exploring new and imaginative ideas. When in fear mode, we may delay taking action or starting projects. We may feel utterly hijacked by procrastination, with a belief (sometimes unconscious) that avoiding the task will protect us from potential failure or disappointment.

Fear of not being perfect can drive us to perfectionism. We might excessively focus on minor details, become paralyzed by the fear of making mistakes, and never complete our projects because they are not 'perfect'. Our fear of challenges or difficult situations can lead us towards 'chronic avoidance' behaviour. We may find ourselves shying away, consciously or unconsciously, from opportunities that could push us towards growth, chances to develop new skills, or confront limitations.

The fear of not 'measuring up' to others can lead us to constant comparison, forgetting we are all unique, with gifts and talents. *Nothing compares to you.* This comparison mind set can undermine self-esteem and deter us from pursuing our own beautifully unique paths. Fear often manifests as negative self-talk, doubting our abilities and reinforcing perceived limitations. This self-sabotaging inner dialogue hinders progress along our path. When stuck in fear of rejection or vulnerability, we can hinder the development of meaningful relationships and actually draw unhealthy relationships into our field. We might withhold our authentic selves to protect against potential hurt, missing out on deep connections and personal growth that might be right in front of us.

Fear often erodes our resilience by discouraging us from facing our challenges. Instead of embracing setbacks as learning opportunities, we may become disheartened and just give up. Fear will keep us in our comfort zones, preventing us from exploring new skills, passions, or areas of interest. This is yet another factor that limits personal growth and prevents us from discovering our hidden talents and living our purpose. To overcome the limitations imposed by fear, we need to cultivate self-awareness, develop coping strategies, challenge negative

beliefs, and gradually expose ourselves to our fears in manageable ways.

Working with plant medicine often induces powerful emotional experiences and a kind of catharsis. This heightened emotional state, combined with the altered sense of time and perspective that psychedelics bring about can help us confront and process deep-seated fears. Many of us experience an increased sense of mindfulness and acceptance during and after psychedelic experiences. This heightened awareness can help us face our fears directly and approach them with a more open, compassionate, and accepting mind-set, potentially reducing the anxiety and distress associated with fears or phobias. Like all experiences in ceremony, this state is not something you can force. It will arise organically if you are ready for the experience.

Many people who journey into other realms with the aid of plant medicine, report an experience of some kind of 'ego death' involving some dissolution of the sense of self, personal identity, personal boundaries, and the normal constructs of personality. This concept of ego death has origins in various spiritual and philosophical traditions. During this experience, people often experience a direct connection with their surroundings, the people in their lives and discover a deeper understanding of existence.

We can experience a lifting of anxiety and fear when we become less preoccupied with our own thoughts, insecurities, and concerns. Ego death can lead to a temporary suppression of 'ego-centric brain processing', enabling some detachment from self-focused thoughts and emotions. As a result, fears and phobias may lose some of their power and intensity. The dissolution of the ego can create an environment where we feel less constrained by the usual mental defence patterns of our conscious mind, the 'guard dog,' and may be more open to exploring and releasing pent-up emotions related to fears.

Expanded states of consciousness can lead to the realisation that many fears are mental constructs and being constructs, may not be as fixed or immutable as they once seemed. This can empower us to

challenge and reframe our fears in more constructive ways. A shift in perspective allows us to view our fears, worries or phobias from a broader and detached viewpoint, often making them less overwhelming and personal.

The 'death experiences' that sometimes occur in ceremonies involves a sense of surrender and acceptance as we let go of our usual control of thoughts and emotions. This surrender can extend to our fears, allowing us to approach difficult feelings with greater acceptance and much less resistance. This can lead to decreased anxiety.

Writing and Reflection Prompts

- In what ways has your fear held you back in the past?

- Are you aware of fear shaping your decisions and life path now?

- How has your fear kept you safe?

- If that fear could speak, what would it say?

- If you could speak to that old fear, what does it need to know, in order to take a new job or a new role in your life?

_____

_____

_____

_____

_____

_____

_____

_____

_____

_____

Looking at Shame

Being shamed in childhood can have a profound and long-lasting impact on our spiritual and emotional well-being. Shame is a powerful and painful emotion that arises when a person believes they are flawed, unworthy, or unlovable.

In a way, many of us were first shamed when were infants with that first slap, the first time we are punished for wetting the bed or having a toileting accident. The first time we are laughed at for being 'wrong' may also be seen as an early 'shame' imprint. All of these 'normal' experiences come with an undertone of shame. They made us feel somehow undeserving, dirty, unworthy, or in some way just not quite good enough. Unfortunately, many of our early life experiences involve a strong sense of shame, shaping our fundamental self-image and beliefs about the world around us. This early shaming can shape our childhood emotional responses, which are often carried over into adulthood. Some early experiences that may induce a sense of shame for one child, may not impact another. We are all born with differing levels of sensitivity, the most sensitive, often suffering the most.

Unfortunately, some parents and caregivers lack communication tools, or have few skills around being present with difficult emotional states, difficult states within themselves, or when seeing these states in others. Many parents these days, have been through their own traumas, and some really struggle to handle the fluctuations of a child's emotions, or their seemingly testing behaviours.

Shaming our children, can shut down what they are doing or expressing, and give us a brief sense of relief or space. We no longer have to face our own demons being reflected back to us by our children,

when we shame and blame. Often, the child is shamed for expressing a 'part of the parent' that the parent is ashamed of. Looking at those who have shamed us, with a lens of compassion, knowing that it's often the pain in the other who is doing the talking, not their authentic self, can take the sting out of a memory.

Having an understanding around how shame has impacted the way we show up in our lives, makes it seem like a pretty important emotional state to get curious about. So what are some of the potential personal emotional and spiritual consequences of shame?

Childhood shame can lead to a deep-seated belief of being somehow inherently flawed, just not okay inside. This can result in low self-esteem and a persistent sense of inadequacy, impacting our sense of self-worth and confidence. Shame tends to distort how we see ourselves. We may develop a negative self-image and see ourselves as unworthy of love, acceptance, and success. Feelings of shame can extend to our spiritual identity. We may develop a belief that we are unworthy of spiritual connection, divine love, or the acceptance of a higher power. This can lead to a sense of spiritual disconnection, or a belief that we are somehow excluded from spiritual blessings.

Childhood shaming has the potential to instil a fear of rejection and abandonment. After being severely shamed, we may avoid forming deep connections out of fear that we will be rejected as soon as our 'flaws are discovered'. Shame has the power to drive us to seek validation through perfectionism. We may believe that by achieving perfection, we can avoid feelings of shame and finally gain acceptance from others. When we are identified with shame-based beliefs, we may isolate, avoiding any potential for judgement or rejection. This isolation can lead us to loneliness, depression, and further reinforce our conscious (or unconscious) negative beliefs.

Shame is closely linked to anxiety and depression. The constant fear of being exposed as flawed or unworthy can lead us to chronic anxiety, while the underlying sense of unworthiness can contribute to feelings of sadness and depression. Carrying the heavy load of deep-seated shame can make it difficult for us to form and maintain healthy relationships. We may struggle to trust others, reveal our true authentic selves, and struggle to be vulnerable due to fear of judgement or rejection. When we carry shame from childhood, we may find ourselves engaging in self-sabotaging behaviours, subconsciously validating and affirming the belief that we are unworthy of happiness or success.

To escape the painful feelings of shame, we might turn to unhealthy coping mechanisms such as substance abuse, self-harm, or a myriad of other destructive behaviours that disconnect, distract or disengage us from what truly matters. If you are using what you know to be unhealthy coping mechanisms, I recommend seeking out additional mental health support through a mode of therapy (such as holistic counselling, somatic therapies etc) in addition to plant medicines.

Shame often prevents us from extending compassion toward ourselves. This lack of self-compassion can drastically limit personal growth and hinder our ability to forgive ourselves for mistakes. When we have been shamed, we might suppress our authentic selves out of fear of judgement. This can hinder our ability to express creativity, opinions, and emotions openly.

Interestingly, research shows that men who have been subjected to serious violence in childhood are more prone to feeling shame. When perceiving shame in later life, they tend to react with aggression towards both sexes. As Psychiatrist, James Gilligan writes:

> Violence and aggression are often preceded by feelings of shame. Shame is one of the strongest and most painful emotions that can affect a person. Instead of directing the anger inwards, against oneself, the aggression is directed towards others. It is a protective mechanism.

Gilligan further proposed that shame is a key, but completely hidden, cause of violence and brought that understanding into his practice of questioning prisoners who had committed murder. When Gilligan asked them why they killed, their answers were often very similar: 'He dissed (disrespected) me. What did you expect me to do?' On the basis of many responses, Gilligan proposed that not only murder, but all violence was caused by what he called 'secret shame,' writing, 'Shame is probably the most carefully guarded secret held by violent men.'

Secrecy implies that one is ashamed of being ashamed: 'The degree of shame that a man needs to be experiencing in order to become homicidal is so intense and so painful that it threatens to overwhelm him and bring about the death of the self, causing him to lose his mind, his soul, or his sacred honour.'

Most people abhor shame, not just the emotion itself, but thinking or talking about it: 'I dreaded shame: I dreaded it more than death... more than all the world.' The destructive power of secret shame can be understood as a feedback loop. Being ashamed of being ashamed is the first step, then, being ashamed of being ashamed of the shame, and ashamed of that, and so on. Shame may also loop with anger: angry that one is ashamed, ashamed that one is angry, and so on. The idea of an unending loop seems to explain how shame, fear, or other emotions might become too powerful to bear and/or control.

Psychedelic medicine has the potential to help us address some of these shame related issues by facilitating a heightened state of self-awareness, allowing us to explore the roots of our shame, understand the origins, and identify how shame has impacted our thoughts, behaviours, and beliefs. The medicine work can help us to access many buried emotions. Traumatic experiences often underlie feelings of shame and psychedelics can help us access repressed memories and emotions, providing an opportunity to process and release these deeply held feelings. With shifts in perception and perspective, we might also gain insights that challenge our shame-based beliefs and offer us new, more compassionate ways of viewing ourselves.

Psychedelic experiences often foster a sense of self-compassion and self-forgiveness. This can counteract the critical self-judgement that often accompanies our sense of shame, allowing us to nurture self-love and acceptance. During medicine work, we might experience emotional releases that allow us to express many bottled up emotions, potentially including shame.

Some of us who journey with the plant spirits report feeling a greater sense of connection to others, nature, or a higher power. This sense of connection can counter feelings of isolation and unworthiness that often accompany shame. Psychedelics have been said to promote neuroplasticity, which is the brain's ability to rewire itself. This could help us break free from entrenched patterns of shame-related thinking and behaviour.

Writing and Reflection Prompts

- Notice when you feel shame and the associated changes in your body language and speech patterns. What is the underlying belief?

- Write down something you have been hiding. Can you speak your words out loud without judgement?

- How do you recognize shame in others?

- How do you create safety with your family members, friends, or workmates so they may feel comfortable expressing what they are ashamed of?

Guilt

When we experience childhood shame, we can often internalise blame for things that were beyond our control. We may carry unnecessary guilt, believing that we caused or deserved the negative experiences that we endured. This is particularly true if we were shamed in the early years.

Naturally, when we are children, we can unconsciously see ourselves as the centre of the universe, everything that happens is 'because of us.' We are at a developmental stage where we are still learning cause and effect, and that not every 'effect' is caused by us. We must also hold our mothers, fathers, and other caregivers on a pedestal of sorts, so that we may have harmony, attunement and attentive caring adults to ensure our basic needs are met. If we were to 'blame' caregivers for the wrongs of our young lives, we could risk relationship ruptures, and disconnection that could also carry a possibility of abandonment and rejection.

Self-blame, shame and the guilt that accompanies these emotional experiences can be 'adaptive' when we are very little beings. The story of 'it's all my fault; it's all because of me,' can help us maintain vital connections for our very survival. Self blame and guilt is certainly less adaptive later in life. But unfortunately, some of the core beliefs around our 'badness' may have already been hard wired. Luckily, all beliefs and a nagging sense of 'guilt' can be shifted. More on this in part three.

Navigating Change

Impermanence is the very nature of life itself. When we fight change, we fight life. Yet many of us are terrified of change, and highly resistant to moving towards the unknown. We live in a world where we are taught to be fearful of any kind of uncertainty, which, when you think about it, is somewhat strange, considering certainty is essentially an illusion. Change happens, whether we like it or not. However, conscious change, and changing un-conscious deeply lodged patterns, means doing a little work, maybe some daily reminders and setting intentions and sometimes a little discomfort (or fun depending on how you choose to look at it).

Our thoughts, beliefs and associated daily actions are an announcement of who we choose to be in this world and seem to 'call in' what unfolds around us. The quantum physics, 'observer effect' would suggest that our inner frequency, where we apply our focus and the nature of the movies we play in our minds – literally impact the physical reality of the materium we move through in our physical world.

Our thinking and imagining, also changes the structures of our brains. When we imagine with focus, our neurology 'thinks' the mind movie is really happening. This is why, for example, hypnotherapy is so powerful and why athletes will practice complex movements and entire events in their imagination and see statistically significant improvements in performance. It is why you can imagine lifting weights and see physical changes in muscle mass.

So, we can either create consciously, or create un-consciously, but we cannot escape the fact that we are always creating. We make our announcements about who we are, while we are 'wide awake and aware', or while metaphorically sleep walking. Once you know a little more of yourself, how you got to where you are, and where you wish to be, it's up to you to decide who you will be in each *now* moment from this point on. Moment to moment awareness, commitment, discipline, and your own will to change are the keys that can unlock as many new doors as you can possibly imagine.

The Importance of Memory

Now is a good time to think about memory. As you revisit your stuff know that your mind is perfectly capable of change. Know that you can change your emotional reactions, even the ones that seem so ingrained that they feel like that have always been that way.

Many people don't realise that memory is a creative process; believing that memory is fixed as though it's a 'real' solid object in the neurons of the mind. Modern neuroscience however, has proven otherwise. If you are interested in expanding your awareness, google 'memory reconsolidation'. The notion that the brain is like a film crew capturing the exact unfolding of the universe around you is easy to believe, but incorrect. We even have gaping holes in our peripheral vision, so the brain 'makes it up' to give us the sense of a full frame of vision. The brain cobbles together information from different regions. When we pull up a memory, we make the data fit a picture. The brain likes to make patterns. If you really want to preserve an event in your brain, never bring it to mind for re-collection.

Just think back to the last time you sat down with an old friend and recalled a shared experience, I bet you both recall the events differently.

After hearing their version, your memory of the event will be recalled slightly differently, with a sprinkling of their insights or stories. Every single time we recollect an event and bring it to the surface, it becomes malleable. We observe it, and it changes, yup, it changes – but the changes are normally so minor we don't notice.

A 'synapse unlocking' takes place when we take a memory file out of the cabinet. This is where we can intentionally amend the memory files with the emotion we want to feel. We then file it back away, and its re-consolidated.

Knowing memory is flaky can be good. We can use this knowledge to 'imprint' *or copy and paste* new emotions that we want to feel on to an old triggering memory. Having an unreliable memory can also work against us if we are in the habit of looking at life through a pair of glasses with dark and gloomy lenses, each time pulling up old memories coupled with emotional states that are equally dark. We may then base our predicted futures on unhelpful past events (hello anxiety).

The brain knows how to feel today, based upon how you have always felt. If you change how you felt, when revisiting a memory, (through many easy processes) you change the brain. You give the brain an option to make a new prediction, from rehearsing a different emotional state.

Activate the Memory
(activity)

1. Activate a memory that might have a little emotional charge, maybe some event that was mildly irritating.

2. Stop yourself from sinking into it too deeply. Just touch upon it.

3. Take a moment to reflect. Do you know, beyond all doubt that your recollection around the event was absolutely truly how you perceived it?

4. How might it have been perceived from any other 'characters' in your memory movie?

5. Would everyone involved have perceived the event how you recall it?

6. Now, with focused attention, bring the mind to a positive feeling state that you would prefer to experience when recalling the memory. If you could wave a magic wand and choose any emotional state at all, what do you want to feel instead?

7. Tell yourself a new story. Think back to that memory, with intention and attention – change the mental images that come to mind. Maybe you would prefer to experience calm, confidence or compassion, maybe another emotional state? Access those resources you would prefer to have inside, imagine you can

'try on' the inner state that you would prefer. Maybe bring to mind a time when you were really calm and confident. Imagine sensing calm and confidence in your body. Who you are, in this desired emotional state? What you are like around others, your community and your friends? How will you be with the characters who are in your inner memory movie while you are in your ideal emotional state? What do you want them to say to you, what do you want to say back? See that memory movie play out differently.

8. Rehearse your new 'resourced memory movie' a few times and see if you notice a difference in how you feel when you bring it back to mind.

9. Remember that the powerful unconscious mind works in metaphor. It is nonlinear and shapes your responses to triggers well before your conscious mind even knows you have been triggered.

By 'resourcing' old triggering memories, we change the emotional intensity they hold. Every time you can stop a negative or uncomfortable feeling loop by remembering something that brings a change in perception, it carves out a new 'choice' for the brain. The brain also generalises. If you were once bitten by a large dog and you weren't able to find regulation after the event; then you may automatically react to all dogs, and react before you can even think about it.

Using this example, you could ask yourself; how do I want to feel around harmless dogs? Maybe calm and open would be more appropriate. So you would really cultivate a calm feeling inside, really

try that on. When 'fully in it' you would imagine yourself in scenes with harmless dogs, all shapes and sizes, maybe walking past them hardly noticing them, maybe patting them, or playing with them. Because the brain generalises positive responses too, when we flex our mental muscles by rehearsing more adaptive reactions with our updated adult tools and resources we carve out new tracks in the forests of our minds.

Personal Reflection

I have had incredible experiences in ceremony, carrying out what seems like 'memory reconciliation' for what feels like many hours – diving into many memories. I revisited old memories where I experienced abuse, and had in depth 'energetic conversations' with the perpetrator. I saw and felt the many lifetimes of layers that led to the perpetrating. I sent my 'child self' the voice she needed, the clarity, the courage and confidence she needed to confront the abuser with a sense of calm and compassion. In my journey, I saw myself saying to the person who abused me: '*I know you are suffering. What is going on inside you that makes you need to do this? Together, let's stop this. Let's heal this.*' The inner theatre, with my new role as director, continued to a point where I could 'hear' and feel his own suffering. From that point of compassion we both healed. Cycles of abuse were stopped.

In this alternate reality, this inner theatre, where the seemingly impossible was possible, the courage of the child actually speaking up, helped my parents become okay with vulnerability. It taught them tools around how to be with uncomfortable emotions and situations. The 'child me' that disclosed, and was heard, seen and believed, brought my own parents close to their parents. It gave them all permission to face their own shadows. It brought them back from a state of distraction and obsession with providing in the material realm. The movie that continued in this medicine journey, gave me a level of compassion for my lineage like I have never experienced before.

My conscious mind 'knows' that the events played out how they did, but my unconscious mind has 'played with this new story in my mind', which is really the only place it exists, and threaded new colours into the tapestry. Now when I pull up the old abuse memory, I am not triggered, not at all. My brain seems to initiate a body state of calm and a generalised sense of compassion.

Ayahuasca, What Is It?

Ayahuasca, sometimes named the vine of the spirit, or One Spirit Medicine, is a medicinal brew, and its main ingredient banisteriopsis caapi, is a giant South American (long stemmed woody vine, rooted in the soul and climbs or twines around other plants) with pale pink flowers, which grows in humid tropical conditions. Ayahuasca is a MAIO inhibitor, (Monoamine oxidase inhibitors) block the actions of monoamine oxidase enzymes. Monoamine oxidase enzymes are responsible for breaking down neurotransmitters such as dopamine, norepinephrine, and serotonin in the brain. This magical vine is cooked, in combination with a catalyst, or synergistic plant. Most often used for this are the leaves of chacruna (Psychotria viridis) chaliponga, chagraponga, and huambisa.

From these plants a brown liquid is produced that is drunk in healing ceremonies led by experienced healers, called *ayahuasqueros* or *curandero/a's*. The effects of the brew will vary greatly depending on the plants used, how they are prepared, in what ratios and how the *curandero* runs the healing ceremony. A number of other complex and mysterious considerations, such as the *Icaros*, sacred chants and songs, vibrations and energies within the healing space that work with the plant spirits will achieve different outcomes and effects.

The use of Ayahuasca has been integral to many shamanic ceremonies and rituals carried out by indigenous communities in the Amazon basin, possibly for thousands of years. In 2010 a pouch (made from three fox snouts sewn together) was discovered in a tomb housing the remains of what Archaeologists believe was a Shaman in Bolivia. The pouch was radiocarbon dated to between 900 and 1170 C.E. It contained the chemical signatures of plants, that are used to brew Ayahuasca.

How did shamans know what plants to brew together to receive the healing from the combination we call ayahuasca? No one really knows for sure just how the shamans of the amazon began to use this combination of plants. But there are some theories. Maybe mother nature, is like a 'super organism' with a big picture in mind, wanting to 'partner' with humanity to nudge our spiritual evolution. Maybe when we are in tune with our intuition, and in harmony with nature, we have stronger communication channels and can actually receive direct guidance from these powerful plant teachers. Perhaps indigenous shamans could perceive guidance directly. Perhaps shamans back in the day observed the Jaguar who would chew the leaves of banisteriopsis caapi, which seemed to improve its sensitivity for hunting, and the indigenous people took it originally for the same reason, then they learnt from there what other plants would teach and serve them in different combinations? We can never know for sure.

Ayahuasca has only recently gained popularity outside of Indigenous cultures. In fact, it was pretty much unknown to the West until the mid-twentieth century when anthropologists first documented its use in South America. One of the first westerners to seek out the medicine was the beatnik William S Burroughs, who was looking for a cure for opioid addiction. But it was not until the Canadian ethnobotanist and popular writer Wade Davis wrote about ayahuasca in his book, *One River*, that the medicine gained a following in the West. Since then there has been a steady growth in the number of people across the world that have sought out the experience of an ayahuasca ceremony.

For millennia, the science, art and magic of healing with sacred plants has been strong throughout Amazonia. The ways of working with the medicine have been passed on orally from generation to generation, and through the plants themselves. The sacred medicine is primarily used to heal, and those of us who engage with this medicine, often experience the following effects:

- **Healing of the physical body:** most people describe a physical purification, clearing, cleansing or even a 'surgery' type of physical process. People often experience vomiting or purging (purging via any of the bodily openings, including the release of tears and sweat).

- **Healing of the mind:** it is not uncommon to experience a kind of regression back to a situation or source of a problem or trauma. People often relive 'emotionally charged' experiences, and gain new insights enabling a process of resolution or closure. Dream-like scenes where personal messages from spirits are received can inspire re-evaluation of our life course and purpose, leaving us with a deeper understanding of why we receive certain messages, and what it is we need to do to fulfil our purpose.

- **Healing the soul:** most people who experience Ayahuasca report some sort of spiritual experience. Unfortunately, it is very difficult to describe the spiritual effects. We simply lack the words.

When we drink this medicine, we are developing a relationship with a powerful spirit, a guide and teacher. We can always call upon this connection, even after the ceremony has passed. When we learn how to listen and feel, we can keep the 'conversation' going. Much of this book is designed to help with this on going process of healing and communicating with spirit, our own spirit, and the spirits of the master plants.

Precautions

Plant medicines like Ayahuasca are not for everyone, and those courageous souls who are looking to journey need to be aware of some risks and 'contraindications'. People who experience high blood pressure, cardiac disease, or liver failure should not consume ayahuasca. Ayahuasca is known to elevate blood pressure levels, so those who suffer from high blood pressure, or cardiac conditions are at risk of complications. Ayahuasca is processed through the liver, so if an individual is in the advanced stages of liver disease, the added stress could be dangerous. Overall, ayahuasca has positive psychological effects, however, some psychological conditions such as schizophrenia or psychosis can be worsened with ayahuasca use. Anyone suffering from these conditions should not participate in ayahuasca ceremonies. Those who suffer from suicidal ideations, dis-associative episodes, or bipolar disorder should ideally heal through other means before engaging with ayahuasca.

Diet, Dieta and Drug Interactions

The typical *ayahuasca diet* is prescribed to manage food interactions with monoamine oxidase inhibitors (MAOIs), a class of medicines often used to treat depression that includes ayahuasca.

Dieta

A *dieta* is a *contract* made between a human and a particular plant spirit. The 'terms of the contract' are decided upon prior to the dieta taking place. What constitutes breaking the contract?: specifics around foods, and timeframes.

Sometimes the motivation to 'do' a dieta comes from some communication or interaction with the plant spirit. Sometimes it is solely decided upon by the person doing a dieta. For instance, in an ayahuasca ceremony, or perhaps in a dream, a plant spirit may present itself and suggest that the person do a dieta with it. It may be that a person feels a connection to a particular plant, perhaps something like Bobinsana, commonly dieted by those visiting the Amazon.

One of the key *terms* of the dieta agreement is its length. Sometimes this is as short as eight to ten days, sometimes a few weeks, months, or even a year or more. The general idea with a dieta is to sacrifice or go without the pleasures of the senses, such as sex and alcohol, or sweet, spicy, salty, or rich foods. For example a person doing a dieta might refrain from all sexual stimulation and alcohol, and commit to eating just potato, rice, specific types of low fat fish and green plantains. Every day, the person doing the Dieta should contemplate the plant they are dieting with, intentionally building a relationship with the plant spirit. They should also drink a tea brewed using the chosen plant throughout the day.

General Pre-ceremony Diet

Before a retreat or ceremony, it is advisable to avoid foods high in tyramine, (a naturally occurring byproduct of the amino acid Tyrosine). MAOIs, and shorter acting *RIMAs (RIMAs like ayahuasca),* block monoamine oxidase, which is an enzyme that breaks down excess tyramine in the body. Aged foods contain the highest level of tyramine, so you want to avoid things like cured meats, aged cheeses, pickled or fermented foods, and alcohol. The warnings about tyramine interaction that are all over the internet are adapted from warnings about interactions with pharmaceutical MAOIs. There are nearly 100 fatalities on record from food interactions with pharmaceutical MAOIs. Unlike pharmaceutical MAOIs, however, Ayahuasca is a reversible (short-acting) MAOI, or RIMA, and there are no confirmed fatalities on record from food interactions with Ayahuasca. Nevertheless, food interactions with Ayahuasca can be highly unpleasant and ruin your experience. They can also be serious if you have elevated blood pressure, or organs under increased stress. But, generally speaking, food interactions are not as serious a risk as those that occur from combining pharmaceutical MAOIs, and other pharmaceuticals with Ayahuasca.

Dietary Advice

The following advice gives you a basic understanding, but it is essential to check in with your retreat organizers regarding diet. To optimise your experience with medicine plants, it is wise to limit for at least seven days prior to arrival at a ceremony or retreat, and seven days after your experience, the following foods:

- Sugars - including artificial sugars or sweeteners (natural sugars found in honey, maple syrup, and fruit are okay)

- Meat

- Animal Fats

- Fermented foods

- Dairy Products (Eggs are okay)

- Caffeine (coffee/tea are okay in moderation)

- Hot spices/peppers

- Processed Foods

- Fried Foods

- Excessive salt

Drug Interactions

These drugs and substances are very dangerous, when taken alongside medicines like ayahuasca. If you are taking any of these medicines, do NOT sit in ceremony. It is ESSENTIAL to disclose any and all medications with your retreat or ceremony organizers.

- MAOI medications

- SSRI's (any selective serotonin reuptake inhibitor)

- Antihypertensives (high blood pressure medicine)

- Appetite suppressants (diet pills)

- Medicine for asthma, bronchitis, or other breathing problems;

- Antihistamines, medicines for colds, sinus problems, hay fever, or allergies (Actifed DM, Benadryl, Benylin, Chlor-Trimeton, Compoz, Bromarest DM or DX, Dimetane DX cough syrup, Dristan Cold & Flu, Phenergan with Dextromethorphan, Robitussin-DM, Vicks Formula 44-D, several Tylenol cold, cough, and flu preparations, and many others) — anything containing dextromethorphan/ DXM or with DM, DX or Tuss in its name, or anything containing pseudoephedrine.

- CNS (central nervous system) depressants

- Vasodilators

- Antipsychotics

- Barbiturates

- Alcohol

Recreational Drugs

Many recreational drugs are dangerous to combine with ayahuasca. You should avoid:

- Cocaine

- Amphetamines (meth-, dex-, amphetamine)

- Ephedrine

- MDMA (Ecstasy)

- MDA

- MDEA

- PMA

- Opiates (heroin, morphine, codeine, and especially opium)

- Dextromethorphan (DXM)

- Nutmeg

- 5-Meo-DMT

There are recorded fatalities from the combination of cocaine with MAOIs and 5-Meo-DMT with MAOIs/ ayahuasca. Illegal or recreational drugs that can potentially be dangerous to combine with MAOIs/ ayahuasca include:

- Mescaline (any phenethylamine)

- Barbiturates

- Alcohol

- Kratom

- Kava

I've said it before, I'll say it again. If you take ANY MEDICINES, discuss in detail with your retreat organizers. People taking medications and failing to disclose, have died,

Food is Medicine

I have some background in cookery. My first role was in a funky vibrant Wellington kitchen with the job description, 'be creative'. We seem to have become disconnected from our environment, where our food comes from and how it's grown and packaged. With this in mind, I've added a series of recipes at the end of this book with a hope that any nutrition in preparation for ceremonies can also be seen as an opportunity to discover new ways of nourishing yourself and loved ones beyond your time working with plant medicines. Although animal foods and eating 'ancestrally' is my personal way, I have included mainly plant recipes in this book.

Things to Ponder

Leading up to your work with plant medicines, I suggest pondering a few of the following things related to eating.

- If I eat animals, where do they come from?

- What are they fed?

- Did they have a right to a good life?

- Are they going through trauma, just being transported to their place of death?

- What kind of energy is stored in their tissues I'm going to ingest? Can I find 'home killed' or wild meat that has died quickly, preferably with an honouring and a giving of thanks?

- Can I support local farmers and growers in my community?

- Am I aware of the impact of chemicals and pesticides?

- How has my food been processed, is it 'real food'?

- If I'm still and give myself time to just be aft er eating, is my body satisfi ed? Is it bloated? Is it 'happy'?

- What beliefs do I have about food? Do I put love, or fear, into what I eat?

Depending on your dieta, or diet instructions, you may (or may not) be consuming garlic, onions, salt, spices or vinegar. Everyone I talk to, and everyone I've sat with has a different way when it comes to nourishing themselves. I like to limit garlic and onions a few days before ceremonies and still have a little in the weeks leading up. My body needs heat and I'm active with low blood pressure, so I tend to have a little salt too. When not drinking medicine, the foundation of my diet is wild meat, fish, and eggs.

Last Minute Tips Before You Book your Trip

Finding the right retreat or Dieta is up to you, this process should not be rushed. It is an opportunity to really use your intuition and inner guidance. Be discerning. We can't rely on what other people say all the time, we need to feel what is right. This goes for everything in life, from discerning truth and alignment around what's on your social media news feed, to finding the right guide in your transformative work. Make sure you are 200% comfortable with the facilitator or shaman you will be working with. Research carefully.

A few things to bear in mind when researching and booking your ceremony:

- I do not recommend sitting alone, or with someone who is simply there pouring medicine into a cup and hoping things don't go wrong

- Look for an experience, and someone with a real passion and sense of purpose in the work they are leading

- Do you want to go into the jungle or seek this work elsewhere (ceremonies are popping up in parts of Europe, Australia, USA and in Canada)? Drinking medicine in the Jungle is a special experience, but not everyone has the capacity for this adventure. And that's okay too

- Look at testimonials, and make sure you feel a sense of connection when reviewing the information available

- Who is the retreat being run by? How long has it been going? What is the lineage of the Sharman?

- Are you looking for a Peruvian style ceremony, or a longer, potentially more 'intense' Brazilian style ceremony (what is your preference)?

- Who is available to answer your questions? Are there people trained at the centre, or ceremony who have additional skills? Is this important to you? (medical staff, counselling support, bodywork, breath work, yoga etc)

- Is there support offered for preparation and integration?

- Where is the actual medicine cooked, and by whom?

- Do you have to 'apply' and then have an interview before being accepted into a retreat? If so, this is good news. It means they are likely to be taking your safety seriously and hopefully all other participants are screened and deemed safe, and ready. All this means there is a reduced chance of drama or negative experiences in the space

- If you choose a few retreats and decide to talk to the organisers, then progress to an interview, make sure you feel supported in asking them questions too

- Does the person interviewing you, ask you about your physical and mental health, your background and what work you have already done on yourself? Do they ask you about medications? Do they ask you why you want this experience? If so, great. You really want to know that everyone in your group is as ready as you are

- Are you feeling heard and respected?

- Watch out for the big ego, salesperson type Sharman (don't get ripped off). No one is your guru. No one is higher, or lower than you are. We are all each other's teachers

- When you are confident you have the right people to work with, make sure you give yourself time to arrange logistics

- Learn about the country you are going to

- Learn a little about the culture, the customs, and the language. Make sure you plan for a comfortable arrival and departure. Land at least a few days before you join a retreat or dieta

- Allow yourself some days of decompression before travelling back home afterwards

- Make sure you are not taking any contraindicated medicines or supplements! And one more time... Make sure you are not taking any contraindicated medicines or supplements!

Packing Tips

For a day ceremony or short retreat in a non-jungle environment bring:

- A head torch with a red light

- Your most comfortable pillows and blankets

If you are heading on a big trip, and staying in the jungle:

- Consider a 'silk liner' sleeping bag for your hut/ tambo

- Fast drying towels and clothing

- A solar power charger

- Pens, pencils, drawing equipment (if that's your thing)

- Musical instruments (if that's your thing)

- Crocks, gumboots, an umbrella, and rain jacket

- A yoga matt (that can be cleaned)

- Mosquito repellent

- Personal first aid items

- Candles, lighter/ matches

- Pegs, hooks and tape could be handy

- Comfy eye mask and earplugs

- Don't pack anything that you are super attached to that could get damaged by mould

- Do bring with you, your open mind, and intentions to allow all healing that is right for you.

Before we move onto part two, I'm going to share a few words I wrote that help me clear my mind and bring me a sense of being grounded. Always find a few ways to 'get grounded' before you travel, especially before you travel to other dimensions!

Prayer of Healing - My Inner Worlds

Underworld

I give compassion to the parts of myself that need to hold onto out-dated or unhealthy patterns that worked to keep me safe during my early years.

I permit myself to drop patterns that may block me from feeling, wanting, having and being fully in this world

I accept what was, is and can be

Like the snake I shed my old skin, I let go and allow myself to feel, to feel even the most subtle energies, that shift me towards my highest good and fullest potential

I now claim my rights to feel, to want, to have and to be here now. I am safe, prosperous, healthy, stable and grounded

I accept pleasure, embrace sacred sexuality, and gracefully feel the full spectrum of emotions with trust and acceptance

Middle World

I give compassion to the parts of myself that are resistant to change, to the parts that feel unsafe in accepting the new

I see clearly how these resistant parts have served me and give them thanks

I give compassion and love to the parts of myself that are afraid of what, and who I might become, after shedding old skin

I give love to the parts of me, who are afraid to step into all that I'm being called to be

With the courage, strength and power of the lioness, I open my heart to love, I choose now to express my voice, and roar

I choose now to express my divine creativity

I invite vitality, spontaneity, strength of will, purpose, self-esteem, and healthy relationships

I choose compassion for all parts of myself and others

I invite balance, self acceptance, clear communication, creativity, resonance and harmony

I claim my rights, to act, to love and be loved, to speak, and be heard

Upper World

I have compassion for the parts of myself that have blocked and doubted, suppressed or pushed down my divine knowing, my intuition, my seeing, spiritual connection and psychic perception

I see that, to survive in this world, some of my most powerful parts were shut away. I forgive myself for forgetting who I really am

Like the eagle and the condor, I now claim back my right to see

Here and now, I pledge to honour my highest knowing

I take back my right to know, to see and feel the truth within myself - and all that presents in my outer world

Aho

Part Two

During your Transformation

Personal Reflection

After numerous ceremonies and retreats I still feel some anxiety before sitting. I still occasionally have the conscious mind throwing negative thoughts my way, such as: *why am I doing this? This is too much! I'm not really needed in this space! Do I really need to be here? What if I can't sing? What if I can't see? What if, what if, what if...* So if you have thoughts that feel a bit scary, thoughts that make you feel like backing out – you are not alone. I remember being incredibly close to pulling out of my first experience at the very last minute but I felt the fear and did it anyway. I'm beyond grateful that I did. My first ceremony was one of the most powerful and transformative experiences of my life. My advice, right before sitting is to plan for a day that feels relaxing to you, taking a walk, meditating, taking a bath, practicing yoga, laying in a hammock, sleeping, reading... whatever it is. Tune in and 'discharge' any pent-up nervous energy.

You can view some of the breathing and movement exercises, and stress reduction tools, in Part Three of this book if you need some ideas.

My Journeys:
the Medicine of Pilgrimage

To me, the pilgrimage we embark upon to reach the magical places in which we journey with the plant medicines, is a medicine in itself. Travel to places that are far from home can be challenging. We learn to embrace foreign languages, new cultures and new environments. This valuable learning builds resilience and self awareness.

My first trip away to journey with Ayahuasca was a challenge. It was not my first time traveling alone, but it was my first trip to Guatemala. I arrived with a good amount of time to explore (something I highly recommend no matter where your destination is), and I travelled straight to Antigua city to spend a few days adjusting. Antigua is a beautiful and colourful baroque city in the Guatemalan highlands, surrounded by three forested volcanoes. I found a wonderful hostel, made some great friends, ate amazing food and explored the surrounding mountains. I climbed a volcano and toasted marshmallows from the heat of lava flowing down the volcanic rocks. This was one unique experience I will never regret or forget!

Following my time in this beautiful little city I found my way to lake Atitlan to spend a week exploring before making my way to the retreat space in one of the lake side villages. Unfortunately, I became very sick, so sick that I could hardly walk. Yet I did not let this deter me from my planned retreat, I felt that perhaps the medicine would help me heal.

Sure enough, after my first sit, my symptoms lifted. I was still exhausted and not moving much, but the intense pain disappeared. My medicine journeys were incredible, life changing and profoundly healing. I received direct messages from my grandmother who was like a second mother to me, but had passed away years before. Her energy was with me throughout the retreat, and she gave me understanding around my life journey and many deep insights around my father (her son). I shared messages with my dad, and what I received from my grandmother was 'spot on' according to him. This entire retreat seemed to be focused upon ancestral healing, death and rebirth. It was hard at times, but just what I needed.

The shamans I sat with in Guatemala were knowledgeable,

professional and held an amazingly safe and supportive space for our group. During this first retreat I connected with some great people, who are still my friends to this day. Upon returning to New Zealand, I managed to connect with more people who were interested in Ayahuasca, doing the inner work and deep transformation. These connections led me to my current partner, right around the time that I found peace just being alone. It was the perfect time to enter a relationship. My partner was invited to spend time with one of his teachers in Peru, and encouraged me to join the small group for a number of Dietas in the Amazon Jungle, and in the Andes.

Due to work and finances, I stayed in New Zealand a little longer than some of our crew and arranged to meet them in a small city called Pulculpa, a starting point for travellers venturing to the smaller villages in the Amazon. I flew into Lima alone, to spend a few days settling in. Settling in, unfortunately, included a few resilience tests. On my second day I was happily cruising the city, looking at maps on my phone, when the next moment, I was looking at my empty hands. A motorbike bandit had just swept my phone from my possession. Suddenly, I was in a foreign country with no access to my travel plans, flights, accommodation or any humans I knew or trusted.

Somehow I managed to make my way back to the Airbnb and hashed out a plan of action. I ended up buying a new phone straight away with the trusty credit card, but seeing as I had two factor authentication active on all my social media and email accounts, it was a complicated, time consuming and highly stressful process regaining access to essential documents and connections. I recommend having a back up plan in case things like this happen while travelling.

Following this first resilience test, I regained composure and committed myself once again to getting grounded and preparing for the next stages of the journey. I flew to Pucallpa to reunite with my partner who had already spent thirty days in the Amazon. I thought Lima was hot, but Pucallpa turned me into a sweaty mess. The day before we were due to venture into the Jungle, we met with the rest of the group who would be travelling with us. All up, there were perhaps thirty people, some going back into the Jungle for round three (like my partner), others going to the Jungle for the first time.

We were on the road before sunrise. In convoy we drove to the river mouth, filed into long, skinny speed boats, then walked to the retreat space. It was hectic, bumpy, uncomfortable, but extremely beautiful. When we arrived we were introduced to the owners and the team who would be supporting us. We were treated to our last feast and shown our *tambos* (little traditional huts with netting for walls), built alongside a weaving jungle path.

The following day, the dieta officially began. During the dieta, we all drank brews consisting of other healing plants, we were fed two meals each day (no salt, sugar, spices or oils - predominantly rice, quinoa, potato and boiled eggs). Every second night we went into ayahuasca ceremonies, for me, these ceremonies were all very powerful. Apart from the music created by the shamans we had the orchestra of (almost deafening) jungle sounds and sometimes torrential downpours. We walked back to our *tambos* in the dark after our ceremonies, wearing our allocated gumboots, taking care to dodge any big spiders, snakes and scorpions.

By the last day, I was feeling like I had undergone a complete transformation, a complete inner clean out and was experiencing a pretty consistent state of awe. The hummingbird was present with me from my first day in Peru, as I had seen three of these magnificent birds on my first day in the middle of the city. When I arrived in the jungle

I had a hummingbird visitor outside my *tambo* each morning, and in most of my medicine journeys, I had the hummingbird come through in my visions.

With the closing of the final ceremony, an early morning session, we broke our dieta and like a stampede, we made our way to the dining hall to enjoy an incredible feast. There is nothing like eating spice and salt after many days of bland food! Exhausted, but happy we began our journey back to the city of Pucallpa. The following day my partner, his teacher, the other facilitators and our little group from New Zealand flew to Cuzco for a few days rest before heading to the Sacred Valley to start another Dieta. Cuzco is a magical city. It was the ancient capital of the Inca Empire, and has been called the Rome of America. I'm not a fan of cities, but the architecture, the markets, the historic ruins, quaint cobblestone streets, amazing restaurants and beautiful people make this city one of the few cities I think I could live in (and not go mad).

The bus ride to the sacred valley took us a few hours, winding through majestic mountains and lush landscapes. A huge contrast to the energy of the jungle, the mountains exuded a different power. We arrived at our retreat centre and settled in, this place was luxury in comparison to the jungle; we had showers, comfy beds and a fireplace in our room. Once again, we shared a little time with the new group and got to know each other before the start of the dieta. I found this dieta to be equally magical, yet very different in the teachings I received.

Following this retreat we made our way, once again to Cuzco where we spent a few nights before the next leg of our journey to the high Andes. My partner's teacher had arranged for us to go on a pilgrimage to stay with a small community, one of a number of communities inhabited by the Q'ero people who are direct descendants of the Inca - those who fled the Spanish invasion. They still live in alignment with nature and the cycles of life in the mountains.

It was a long journey, winding up treacherous mountain roads. We were warmly greeted by the community who had generously offered to host us, moving their families around to accommodate us in their traditional dwellings made from stone, mud, bricks and the occasional object - like a shoe plugging a hole in a wall, or an old jandal acting as a gate hinge.

We enjoyed the festivities and partook in traditional ceremonies, honouring the spirits of the land and the ancestors. We shared stories, music, dance, homebrew and traditional foods. Time flew by. After a few nights immersed within this inspiring, wise community, we travelled on by bus, and then horseback to a small collection of buildings near the foot of Ausangate Mountain with a few of the Q'ero community leaders.

In this sacred setting, we partook in a fire ceremony with more singing and dancing, and then went to bed early so that we could rise before the sun. Upon waking, we walked to a special part of the mountains to meet the glacial river whereby we would partake in a cleansing ceremony with the Q'ero elders. After this, it was time to journey back into 'civilisation', to say farewell to some of our group, and to prepare for the next adventure. The experience in the mountains, living simply and learning from the community was a truly humbling, a reminder of how we can harmonise with nature when we live in presence, peace and trust.

Because we love mountains, and being in Peru, we simply could not fail to do some hiking, and our next mission was a five-day trek to Machu Picchu. Crazily we planned this next adventure to take place one day after our return from the Q'ero community. It was a marathon effort just getting ready for the hike, ensuring we had plenty of snacks, coca leaves, warm clothes, and a little Wachuma for the road. It was a 4:30 a.m. start, but we made it, and soon discovered we had the coolest tour guide in the country.

The Salkantay trail is said to be challenging, but we found that we were well prepared after all our hiking in New Zealand, and a good amount of time in Cuzco prepared us for the high altitudes. We then went on to explore Huacachina, an oasis town with crazy dune buggies and dune boarding, The Nazca Lines, Arequipa, (the white city), Puno and Lake Titicaca. If you have the capacity to spend a few extra days, or weeks, away from your home country, I recommend making the most of it.

Other Medicines

Depending on your hosts, you can expect to be offered a number of medicines during your retreat, and within the ceremony itself. So that you have a little more insight around these medicines, I have added a little information about the most common medicines below.

Rapé

Rapé (pronounced ha-peh) is a sacred medicine used by various indigenous tribes in the Amazon rainforest. It is also known as hape, hapé, or snuff. Rapé is made in a ceremonial setting, from a combination of tobacco leaves and other sacred plants ground into a fine powder. The medicinal plants used will vary depending on the intention around how the blend will be used and for what purpose. In ceremonies, the resulting powder is blown into both nostrils one at a time, using a pipe called a Tepi. Traditionally, the shaman or an assistant will offer rapé throughout your ceremony for a number of different reasons.

I find Rapé useful in 'cutting the thoughts,' it brings me into my body and away from mental chatter, so it's very useful right before drinking that first cup of medicine. Certain types of Rapé are used to help us to 'bring on the purge', if the nausea is intense, and we know something needs to come out, but it just wont come, Rapé to the rescue! Rapé can be used if we are having a 'big process', stuck emotionally or mentally in a dark loop and just can't get out, again, Rapé to the rescue!

In general Rapé is believed to have various effects, including:

- **Cleansing and purification:** some indigenous cultures use rapé to clear energetic blockages, cleanse the mind and body, and remove negative energies or entities

- **Mental clarity and focus:** Users often report enhanced mental clarity, heightened awareness, and improved concentration after using rapé

- **Connection and communication:** rapé is sometimes used as a tool for connecting with higher realms, spirits, and ancestors. It is also used to facilitate communication and understanding within tribes and communities

- **Grounding and centring:** despite its stimulating effects, rapé is believed to have a grounding and calming influence, helping us to feel more connected to the Earth and our surroundings

- **Physical effects:** some users experience physical sensations, such as a warming or tingling sensation, as the rapé is blown into the nostrils

It's important to note that using rapé is deeply intertwined with the spiritual and cultural practices of the indigenous tribes that have been using it for generations. For these communities, rapé holds great significance and is a sacred medicine. It is not a recreational substance.

Sananga

Sananga is another traditional Amazonian medicine that comes from the roots of a plant species belonging to the Tabernaemontana and Maytenus family. It is used by various indigenous tribes in the Amazon rainforest. Like rapé, sananga is commonly used in ceremonies.

Sananga is prepared by extracting the juices from the roots of the plants through a process of maceration. These juices are then bottled and applied directly to the eyes using a dropper. The process of applying sananga to the eyes is referred to as 'eye drops' or 'eye medicine.' Although not psychoactive, per se, many Shamans say that Sananga helps to bring on, or intensify the visions while in ceremony.

The application of sananga to the eyes can be intense and cause a little (or a lot) of discomfort depending on the strength of the batch. When we use Sananga, we can expect to experience stinging, burning or tearing, which typically subsides after a short period. The discomfort is considered part of the purifying and cleansing process.

The traditional uses of sananga include:

- **Eye health and vision:** indigenous tribes believe that sananga has the ability to cleanse and detoxify the eyes. It is used to improve vision, remove energetic blockages, and enhance clarity of perception. People who use sananga often report improved visual acuity and sharper colours

- **Spiritual and energetic cleansing**: just like other Amazonian medicines, sananga is believed to have energetic and spiritual cleansing properties. It is used to remove negative energies, attachments, and emotional or psychic blockages

- **Purification**: sananga is often used in purification ceremonies or rituals, helping individuals prepare themselves mentally, physically, and spiritually for important events, ceremonies, or challenges

- **Heightened awareness**: some people who use sananga, report increased sensory perception, focus, and a heightened state of awareness after application

- **Connection with ancestors and spirits**: like many traditional medicines, sananga is used to facilitate communication with ancestors, spirits, and the unseen world. It is believed to open channels of communication and connection to the spiritual realms.

Kambo

Kambo is a traditional medicine developed by the Panoan-speaking groups of the southeast Amazon. It is a waxy substance collected by scraping the skin of an Amazonian tree frog, Phyllomedusa bicolor. Yes, the rumours are correct. Kambo makes you feel uncomfortable. This could explain why Kambo is also known as an 'ordeal medicine'. People don't take Kambo to have fun. They take it to cleanse, heal themselves and oftentimes prepare themselves for work with medicines like Ayahuasca. Kambo is often used in conjunction with ayahuasca, as Kambo can help to optimise its effects and it's absorption. The vasodilation (opening of the blood vessels) created by the peptides phyllomedusin and phyllokinin also increase the permeability of the blood-brain barrier.

The Kambo ceremony takes into account the discomfort that is expected, and is structured with the intention to provide a safe setting for what can be a challenging experience. Generally speaking, those of us who choose to participate in a Kambo ceremony, know what awaits. When meeting Kambo, there are no distractions from the experience, and there shouldn't be. Full presence and respect is everything. As with so many of these medicines, you may not get what you want, but you will get what you need.

Like with ayahuasca, when taking Kambo, preparation is necessary, and the cleansing process begins well before the ceremony. Most Kambo practitioners recommend fasting for 10-12 hours before use. Recreational drugs and alcohol are not to be consumed for at least 24 hours before, and after a ceremony. It is generally recommended that participants consume 1-2 litres of water before the ceremony begins.

During a ceremony, a Kambo practitioner applies the Kambo to participants, by using small burns made on the skin. These small burns are known as 'gates,' the small burns allow the Kambo to enter into the bloodstream quickly. The immediate effects of Kambo are intense, pretty unpleasant but tend to last no longer than 30-40 minutes.

You can expect to experience a rise in temperature, sweating, shivers, and dizziness, your heart rate tends to become rapid, sometimes reaching more than 190 beats per minute. Your blood pressure may rise or fall dramatically. Some people report a burning sensation, or tingling, like electricity that starts from the points and spreads through the body. Nausea is generally unavoidable with Kambo and purging is highly likely by vomiting, defecation, or both. You may also experience a feeling of pressure in the torso, neck and head, stomach pain, inflammation or pressure around the throat, a dry mouth, blurred vision (or even temporary blindness), numbness, difficulty moving, and numb, swollen lips and tongue.

When these initial biological effects have worn off and the heart rate has returned to normal, the body will transition into a more restful state.

Following the ceremony, you may feel increased physical strength, heightened mental clarity, alertness, and sharpened senses. These after-effects may take a day to materialise or they could be immediate. They also tend to include a consistently elevated mood, decreased stress, and enhanced focus.

One of Kambo's most exciting potential applications is the treatment of cancer. Dermaseptin B2, a peptide found in Kambo, has been shown to inhibit cancer cell growth by more than 90%. This peptide also penetrates cells and actively destroys cancer cells. Dermaseptin's are powerful antibiotics and antivirals. They have been found to be rapidly and irreversibly effective against a wide range of parasitic microorganisms; they're also entirely non-toxic to healthy mammalian cells. Combined with their ability to cross the blood-brain barrier, the peptides in kambo are very promising for conditions like Cryptococcal meningitis in patients with late-stage HIV. Dermaseptin B2 destroys the filamentous fungi that opportunistically infect AIDS patients.

Since adenoregulin, a chemical found in Kambo, affects the binding of agonists to adenosine receptors—instrumental in the permeability of the blood-brain barrier, Kambo may be useful in the development of treatments for Alzheimer's disease, depression, and strokes. Anecdotal evidence supports kambo's use in depression treatment, anxiety, and addiction. There's also compelling anecdotal evidence for kambo's

effectiveness in the treatment of chronic fatigue syndrome (CFS). The deltorphins and dermorphin present in kambo have analgesic effects comparable to the body's own pain response of beta-endorphin release. They're also stronger than morphine without the same level of respiratory depression, tolerance potential, and withdrawal symptoms. Phyllokinin, another chemical present in Kambo, may be useful in the treatment of hypertension, having been shown to lower blood pressure more effectively than other polypeptides. Other conditions that may benefit from kambo include chronic pain, Parkinson's disease, vascular problems, hepatitis, diabetes, rheumatism, and arthritis. So, although Kambo is not fun, it's an amazing medicine, and I highly recommend the experience, if you are medically fit for it and it is available.

Part Three:

Diving Deeper
After Transformation

Personal Reflections

I have had many sudden and clear insights during ceremonies over the years. I have had for example messages from ancestors around deep traumas, and how these traumas have impacted my immediate family and my personal life lens.

On one occasion, in my visions I was taken to Ireland. I was standing with my Irish ancestors and feeling their pain, their desperation, their suppressed voices. I felt and sensed the depth of the hurt from their impoverished situation, the debt enslavement, war and famine. I felt compassion, and a sense of relief. Suddenly, I could feel deeply, the root of my need to control certain aspects of my life, the roots of the fears, especially the fear of 'not having enough'. Many of my wounds that I struggled to understand all suddenly made sense. They were not just *mine* but passed down through generations. In this short moment, I was presented with a significant opportunity: to find peace and heal ancestral traumas by allowing myself to fully feel the emotions and sensations carried within my DNA, to let the tears come, and experience emotions maybe repressed for generations.

I have also received very clear and sudden insights around relationships that drained my energy, and how to lovingly cut ties (physically and energetically) without blame or resentment. I discovered early on that it's very helpful to have a supportive friend 'on call' who has had similar experiences in the days and weeks that follow deep work. I have also found it very useful to take the contact details of those who have shared space with me in ceremony. Having these connections in place, for times when we are struggling or having a rough day, is priceless.

So now that we have considered preparations, explored emotions and body awareness, looked at how fear, shame and guilt can hijack our minds, talked about what to expect and how to navigate your ceremony or retreat environment, it's time to take a deeper dive into the process of leaving the environment in which your transformation has begun to take place. The act of leaving a plant medicine retreat can be challenging. With any, and all, transformational experiences, once the initial 'chapter of transformation' has come to a close, we can be left feeling uneasy around how to truly ground, or land into, a 'new self'. The likelihood of maintaining the inspiration to truly embody spiritual insights, improve health, improve significant relationships in our lives, and make general life changes, improves when we take time to reflect, heal old wounds and understand unwanted patterns.

During periods of deep work and in the days that follow, early life events may come up for us to look at once again. Often, what surfaces has previously been 'shut down', repressed, blocked, minimised, justified or just ignored. The re-emergence of memories into conscious awareness through the medicine work, opens an opportunity to 'review' these 'old wounds', allowing them be seen with a fresh lens. They can finally be processed, fully understood, forgiven, accepted and integrated.

When we delve into other realms with the aid of plant medicines, we can expect to experience or perceive encounters with spirit guides, past lives, our higher self, 'off world' entities, angels, demons, teachers and more. You may be shown the wounds of your ancestors and your present day loved ones. You may experience insights around how these wounds or traumas are connected to your own wounds and traumas. You may gather insights around how to heal, not only yourself, but your past self, your ancestors, family, and even your wider community. These insights may lead to relief, inspiration, and motivation to make big changes.

We can experience insights around new projects, career changes, our life purpose and direction. These insights can feel incredibly exciting, inspiring and motivating. On the flip side, they may also feel very scary and challenging, especially if we apply pressure upon ourselves to make dramatic changes immediately. It can be helpful to remember that 'good things take time.' Change does not have to happen instantly. It can be more sustainable if we move gently, exercise self-compassion and take one step at a time. You may feel elation and excitement, but you may also experience a sense of overwhelm, anxiety, confusion and panic. Perhaps, you will feel that it's all 'too much'. In times of overwhelm, it's vital to remember that we all have tools, like breath and movement (more on that later).

Remember the love of the medicine. Remember to be gentle with yourself. Time is a human construct, so remember to relax and allow changes to flow in a nonlinear way. The only rush is what we create in our minds. Trusting that moments of change will come organically, or sometimes unexpectedly, seems to help with the common experience of overwhelm.

It is true that those of us that make this journey into the spirit world, may start beating ourselves up for not *'seeing it all sooner'*, for not *'doing enough'*. We may experience an inner dialogue that sounds something like, *'I can't deal with all of this,'* and other forms of mind clutter. The jumbled self-talk can sometimes lead us towards the experience of shutting down, guilt, or shame. Sometimes it feels like the ego is trying to claw its way back into a position of power, and that's okay. The ego is not evil. The ego has kept us all safe. It's been a great teacher. There is room to allow for co-existence between the parts that feel 'egoic' and the parts that feel like a 'higher self'.

We don't have to walk away from a retreat or ceremony with all the answers, fully healed, one hundred percent upgraded, fully transformed and charged up. One step at a time is how we climb the mountain, while hydrating, breathing deeply, resting, and loving ourselves to the best of our abilities throughout the difficult climb. We are only given what we can handle, even the hard stuff. When transforming ourselves it's certainly not just sunshine and rainbows. We must expect to experience an entire orchestra of emotions: euphoria, peace, oneness, but also, terror, dread, and even a form of death, death of old ways, old beliefs, and aspects of the ego. When the uncomfortable emotions rise up, it's important to refrain (as much as possible) from self-judgement, running from feelings or seeking distractions.

Initial Reflections, the Real Work Begins

It can be helpful to remember that everything we experience that is seemingly catalysed, or brought up by plant medicines has always been somewhere within, but possibly lying dormant. It can be easy to slip into a 'victim' or depressive state when tough stuff comes up as it is hard work to take responsibility and look deeply within. Those of us who do this work can learn to look at experiences with a broad, metaphorical, and compassionate lens and to walk forward in life, empowered, not as victims. Rather than falling into a state of victimhood, we can learn to hold compassion for the wounded parts of ourselves and uncover new healthy ways to sit with, and process, discomfort and triggers. When working with plant teachers, it's also not uncommon to receive insights around life direction and goals, remember, baby steps.

Deeper Dives Writing Prompts

During your recent transformational experiences did you receive any sudden, clear lessons or teachings? Note down some major themes, lessons or teachings.

_____

_____

_____

_____

_____

_____

_____

- Are emotions present when you consider major themes, lessons or teachings that have come up?

- How would you describe the dominant emotions?

- Are you aware of body sensations alongside any emotions?

- How would you describe them?

_____

_____

_____

_____

_____

_____

- Did you receive new insights around what you need to focus more or less energy on?

- List ways that you can apply these new insights in your daily life

_____

_____

_____

_____

_____

_____

_____

Who can you call upon to remind you of these insights and desired actions? Close friends who have been through their own transformation? A trusted therapist? People who you have shared time with while on your retreat or ceremony?

_____

_____

_____

_____

_____

_____

What manageable steps can you take to begin to manifest new goals, directions and higher aspirations? Notice any negative 'self-talk' that comes up around new goals and directions (*I'm not doing enough, I can't, or I'll change when*).

_____

_____

_____

_____

_____

Play negative self-talk back in your mind, in a voice from a character that makes you laugh, maybe a chipmunk voice, any funny cartoon. Do you notice a difference?

_____

_____

_____

_____

_____

_____

- What are some words you can imagine saying to people you care about who are navigating big changes?

- Imagine saying encouraging words to yourself and note down any changes in how you feel

_____

_____

_____

_____

_____

_____

_____

_____

- Recall a goal inspired during your recent work. When you have achieved it, what will it do for you?

- Note down all the things that will change.

- When you have all that, how will you feel?

- Note down all the feeling states you can.

_____

_____

_____

_____

_____

_____

_____

_____

- What will that do for you as a person? Who will you be?

- When you are *that kind of person*, what will be important to you?

- Who are you *being*, in your family, your work, your community?

- How are you outwardly expressing your values and purpose in daily life?

- Note down all the words that relate to your new way of being

_____

_____

_____

_____

_____

_____

_____

_____

_____

_____

Circle the words you have written down that speak to a core identity, words that really spark you up inside.

Looking at all the words, create a sentence, a personal mantra, that will motivate small daily steps towards naturally and organically achieving the goal.

Start the mantra with:

I am becoming (e.g. more confident every day, more in tune with my needs, someone who sets boundaries)

_____

_____

_____

_____

_____

As I become

_____

_____

_____

_____

_____

I embody

_____

_____

_____

_____

_____

(Additional positive words or a sentence that motivates you towards your new identity, and therefore the natural progression towards your goals)

Play around with closing the eyes, and 'trying on' the goal with all the senses. Notice the feelings and any changes in the body, breathing and posture. Does it feel motivating? What do you notice?

Connection is Medicine

Consider how you can connect more deeply with:

- Nature and music

- Community

- People in your life that bring you a sense of love, wholeness and harmony

List ideas around how you can regularly connect with nurturing energies

_____

_____

_____

_____

_____

_____

_____

_____

Can you imagine new ways to connect with your body, your creativity, and your intuition?

Who, or what do you need to start removing from your life that brings you down?

Who, or what do you need to bring into your life?

_____

_____

_____

_____

_____

_____

A gentle reminder: while you are 'landing' and going through some initial reflections, working hard to process your 'stuff', it can be helpful to remember that 'connection' is medicine. The safe connections and relationships we build in a retreat space, open the way for us to look within, be honest with ourselves and those around us, and allow us strength to do the work. If possible, keep in touch with those you shared space with while you continue to process your insights.

So, now we have navigated some initial reflections, we can begin to cover some specific topics. Some may feel more relevant than others. And you should feel free to skim over the parts that aren't important to you.

Inner Processing

Early life events, highly charged memories, difficult life situations and relationships (with parts of ourselves and others) often come to the surface when we carry out deep transformative work. In the time that follows retreats and ceremonies some contemplation of charged memories can be very useful and also pretty challenging. By making peace with highly charged memories and building a greater understanding of them, we can actually find more space to move forward, to find compassion, forgive ourselves and others and to let go.

Naturally, new ways of seeing ourselves, our past traumas and current reality can feel confronting and overwhelming. We can suddenly see previously hidden, wounded parts of ourselves that need our attention and compassion. The emotional charge and body sensations that can come up alongside our 'stuff', seemingly out of nowhere, can feel terrifying, but we may also view this 'charge' in the system as exciting and illuminating. An entire range of feelings can show up. And all these feelings are okay.

Personal Ceremony Journal

Shadows of the forest emerge from all aspects of the kaleidoscope, the kaleidoscope that is my visual field, a visual field now connected with the mother of all creation. I see roots, roots connected to the core of the earth, an earth that exists primarily as an energetic field, an energy field in constant motion, moving and inspiring us through our senses to create. She says, 'create beauty, create love, harmonious sound and art, create so that I may experience creation through you and with you'. The great mother of all creation wants us to co-create, but not just mindless creations, creations in alignment with our highest good, and the highest good of all that is.

She wants to dance to our music, her music that comes through us when we listen. She wants us to dance too. She wants to help us heal through the outward expression of the love she gives, and the lessons she shares. She wants us to spread the love by healing ourselves and loving without condition. She dances in technicolour spirals, threads, webs of sound, light rising through her roots within the shadows of the kaleidoscope forest, light weaving reality together with the rhythms of the sounds.

I see another dimension of forest beings, mini robots with huge eyes and tiny beaks, layering on top of each other, superimposing, dancing and swimming through the vast matrix, the energy fiend of this infinite dimension, normally just beyond reach, but forever inside and surrounding me. The beings are in a magical communion with sound, the sounds of the jungle and the Icaros, light beings dancing to the sounds, moving with every slight shift in frequency.

They ask me to lie down and surrender with love and trust. Then they start to work on my body, they pick, pull, and weave in and out. Gently fixing the parts of my body that have been physically damaged, then move to the energy centres and clear emotional blockages. I'm asked to sit, to roll over, to lie down and sit again. Then, very clearly, they say, 'open your mouth'. It's bizarre, but I do it. Suddenly, I see and feel ribbons of light flood my throat, clearing and cleaning the parts of me too broken to speak, to have a voice. Too afraid to sing.

Choking at birth, fighting for breath and life, then ripped away from warmth suddenly cut from the life source. So many parts of me, unconsciously shamed into silence. So many old emotions rise to the surface to be fully felt, embodied, experienced and cleared by these mysterious beings of light, with the energy and presence of the mother of all creation. The overwhelming sensations, rolling over me and through me, sensing the 'shame' of being alive, sensing that old shame, then sensing it lift, lift and float away into the void.

I'm told that the time is now. Surrender to joy. You deserve it. Trust this body, soften, let go. Listen, listen, listen. Drop into the heart, the heart always knows. Nurture yourself. Don't beat yourself up anymore. You don't need to earn the right to live your day, your day is a gift without conditions. You have been through more than enough. Live.

Life Events – Writing Prompts

During your transformational experience, have any emotionally charged events, situations or dynamics from childhood shown up in your awareness?

_____

_____

_____

_____

_____

_____

_____

- Has awareness come up for you around needs that were *not* met in your life?

- Have you experienced strong emotion around missing out on what you truly needed during key moments of your life journey?

- Can you name the emotions?

- Did you also experience body sensations alongside any emotions?

- Use this space to express in words, what might need to be expressed.

Visualization Exercise

Shut your eyes, and tune into your imagination. Allow yourself to float back into the sensations you experienced in the medicine space, letting go of the critical mind. Maybe imagine that, as your body surrenders and relaxes, your mind can float up and out... observing with a relaxed open focus. Let go of self-judgements and limitations. Imagine 'the child' version of yourself on a small screen in your minds eye. Perhaps you can imagine seeing a scene from childhood, an impactful scene, as if it's on a TV screen at your feet.

Ask your unconscious mind, 'What did I need back then, that I have now, what resources do I have that would have made that scene play out differently"? Really feel what those strengths, resources and characteristics or traits feel like now. Notice who you are with these resources (maybe confidence, compassion, wisdom, or a strong voice). How do you stand, speak, and act towards others and yourself? In this resourced state, knowing what you know, imagine you can offer that child the resources that you have now, as an adult.

Imagine sending those resources and support in your mind. When you feel those resources have been embodied by that child down on that screen in your minds eye, just watch that scene play out differently. Perhaps the child stood up for themselves, or got themselves out of a situation. Play around with the mental movie in any way that feels good.

Once you have imagined that child version of self 'succeed' and feel empowered, imagine floating down and merging with that child version of yourself, bringing the integrated version of yourself back into this moment. Notice and reflect upon any changes in how you feel.

The conscious mind may know that this new 'mind movie' is not how the event occurred, but as i've said many times, the unconscious mind works in metaphor. New neural pathways are created through both real and imagined experience. By remembering past events and imagining new future memories we change our brains.

Some people, see new perspectives during transformative work and following visualization activities. Perhaps you saw new perspectives that open doors to new conclusions, or interpretations, around parts of your life journey so far? If so, take a moment to write any new insights.

_____

_____

_____

_____

_____

_____

_____

_____

_____

_____

_____

Back to the Mind Gym

While contemplating, if it feels right for you, choose one emotionally charged memory. Tune into body sensations and your emotions as you sit with your memory and just notice what comes up. Allow your mind to totally relax, perhaps stare at one point in front of you, and as you do, relax and soften your gaze. Without moving your eyes or head, start to notice the space around the point you are staring at. Without moving your eyes or head, just notice more and more space around that point. Notice as far as you can, without losing sight of that starting point. With your focus open and relaxed, suggest to yourself, 'my mind can totally relax, along with my body'. With this soft gaze, and open focus, just notice the sounds in the room, what can you smell? Dropping your jaw, notice what space feels like in your mouth, the space between your mouth and the back of your eyes, just notice the space. With a relaxed nervous system, does that memory or 'inner charge' change? Write down any insights or journal about any changes you notice in your body during this 'open focus' exercise.

_____

_____

_____

_____

_____

_____

Healing our Inner Child

Traumas don't always have to be big events. Seemingly common occurrences can wound us. For example, experiencing a lack of connection or assurance in challenging times can be damaging on many levels. These experiences may form limiting beliefs that (once seen and acknowledged) can take time to fully unpack and reprogram.

When we don't feel seen or heard, when we don't receive the emotional or physical support we need in our early years, we may internalise that as our fault. We are obviously not 'worth' it, not important enough to be noticed and held. This early 'meaning making' is mostly unconscious. But as mentioned previously, on a positive note, it gives children a way to maintain attachments with key caregivers.

Very early on, during the years we cannot clearly recall, before we can fully express ourselves, we don't blame our parents. We very rarely risk expressing emotions that could rupture a bond we are dependent upon. Our parents are like gods to us in the formative years, so we create stories to keep them on the pedestal. Even if that means that we take on shame and guilt, internally making a lack of attuned presence 'our own fault', due to our imperfections.

If you are sitting with a realisation that perhaps your unmet needs damaged your sense of worth, and 'right to be' in the world, now is a great time to give yourself some space to offer love and compassion to that child inside, a part we often judge without even being aware of it. It is a part of ourselves that does not feel worthy and can struggle with creating boundaries, saying no, expressing needs and finding a voice. Now we are adults, we can heal these aspects of self, and learn to affirm our worth in the world without fear of abandonment.

Looking into who helped us when we were under stress in our early years can be very illuminating. The energy that met us, or failed to meet us, when we needed unconditional love, attunement and presence helped to build our foundation of self, how we see our place in the world and how our unconscious mind codes information.

Getting Curious About Beliefs

When we are doing inner work, participating in ceremonies, retreats and working with medicines, we often find ourselves peeling back many layers, including unravelling and exposing core beliefs. It can sometimes be tricky to follow the threads, to find the roots, examine them and decide if certain beliefs still feel like truth, serve us, or limit and harm us. If we discover that some old beliefs are no longer feeling true, or useful, how can we gently foster a letting go process, a reprogramming of sorts? How can we start building new stories that serve us and actually help us grow and evolve?

It all starts with daily practice, the work of self-awareness, catching our thoughts and getting curious every time we notice a thought that feeds an unwanted pattern. When we get attentive and curious, we can bring forward a practice of labelling thoughts as they arise, thoughts that aren't *us*, but stories we play about ourselves in our minds.

Personal Reflection

A belief that came up for me to examine in ceremony was the belief, or story, that I'm not important or a priority in relationships. The very first time I felt this sense of being disregarded and unimportant, was when I was just a child. My needs were not truly seen or felt. My first experience of institutions terrified me. I did not feel safe in pre-school, or school. I was bullied from day-one and did not learn in the same ways as others. I was abused at six. No one close to me noticed the changes within me, or the changes in how I engaged with the outside world. Somewhere along the way, I unconsciously made this mean that I was not worth being seen or listened to, that I may as well be out of my body. I may as well be invisible. All this impacted my ability to trust others, and trust myself.

Plant medicine once gave me the lens of my mother. I was suddenly thrown through the web of time and reality. I melted into a consciousness within my mother in a past timeline. While sharing this reality, I could feel her physical and emotional experiences, when I was in her womb. I was the observer, and the participant. I was energetically existing in the past and present to help shift the notes of our relationship in the present. I sensed and experienced, with all my cells, her emotions, her fear, her anxiety, her excitement, the full range of emotions while carrying me in her womb. I truly felt and experienced her inner battles, her love, but also the pressure. I could feel her own wounds and how they impacted her beliefs about her self and how these beliefs shaped her.

I felt the expectations from society to be a 'good mother' but also the impossibility of surviving without two parents working, working so much they didn't have the capacity to always truly see their children and hold them as they needed to be held. I saw how society has been manipulated over hundreds of years, structured in order to create these disconnections and traumas. How traumatised children are easy to shape and manipulate. I felt the progressive disempowering and dividing of the genders and races, the shaming of women for wanting to nurture, and the shaming of men when one job is not enough to be a 'provider.' All the while there was an illusion of more and more material 'necessities', more things that must be acquired in order to fit into the world and to be happy. To attain the American dream, (the illusion or delusion), just get into debt slavery, 'have it all' and buy happiness. I saw this machine-like system as an entity, creating disharmony and chaos, feeding upon fear. Seeing the madness of the structures surrounding me, I suddenly became free. If I'm not afraid, I can starve the beast!

My New Story

I had held onto this idea that I was a burden, not planned, not really wanted, always in the way, and just another job to deal with at the end of the busy workday. I felt not fully seen for who I was, and really, not worth seeing or hearing. In reality, my parents loved me dearly, and still do. I was indeed a priority, but there were blind spots. They did not see how a lack of presence would translate into a child's core beliefs around 'not being enough'. Their way of putting the kids first, was providing physical needs, making money, not necessarily being physically and emotionally present.

But they were full of love and desperately wanted their children to be safe, and to have all their needs met. The shape and structure of society was not their fault and certainly not the fault of my mother, so why all the resentment? I had to change the story and forgive. Our early life experiences and 'emotionally charged' situations can shape the way that we see the world, the stories we tell ourselves, and can shape our deeply rooted beliefs.

More Self-Inquiry - Writing Prompts

Contemplate a 'charged' early memory that creates a 'trigger' within, a memory that may have come back to you during a recent or transformational experience.

- Who did you tell when that triggering situation was unfolding? If nobody, how would you explain that?

- How would a child that you know, in a similar situation feel?

- Who would you want your own child to talk to?

- If your 'child part' that was suffering and did not talk to parents or caregivers, what was the reason?

- Can you imagine what you might have made that mean? *E.g.; I'm not a priority, I'm not good enough?*

- Are there aspects of your life now, where you are perhaps still living from that old belief?

_____

_____

_____

_____

_____

_____

_____

_____

You can choose to take that triggered feeling and change it using activities in the previous section, perhaps seeing that inner child on a black and white screen. Find your current strengths and resources and imagine sending those down to that child part. Perhaps, give that sensation a symbol and imagine it vanish, then bring in a better feeling state.

Now revisit another emotionally charged event/ situation/ dynamic that may have come up for you in your recent transformative work.

- What beliefs did you make about yourself because of a 'traumatic or highly charged event?

- In your transformational process, did any other teachers show up and offer insight around your core beliefs? Actual humans, or entities showing up in your mind's eye?

- Perhaps your transformational experience has given you the 'eyes of an observer' or 'other participant' in a life situation from the past. If you were looking through any other lens, other than your own, (shaped by your naturally limited experience), are there alternative stories, meanings and beliefs that might hold truth? E.g. 'My parents didn't care', or 'My parents were coping with their own trauma's, pressures and stressors, loved me and cared deeply, but did not have capacity to hold space for me.' Notice any changes within as you offer your mind new ideas.

_____

_____

_____

_____

_____

_____

_____

_____

_____

_____

Our Many Parts
Personal Reflection

I have seen many addictive patterns, my inner fire fighters, in ceremony. I have seen the first moments they came to life. These patterns of behaviour came into being, during a stage of my life where they helped me survive. I was a child, and children don't have a full emotional toolkit. I experienced a wave of compassion for this rather extreme and self-destructive part. Compassion replaced the usual shame and guilt, compassion replaced the shame that this part even existed and persisted in times of stress. I saw this part's goodness, the determination, the motivation and inner 'grit'. I then asked it if it would like to apply those qualities in healthy ways, in new and constructive areas of my life. This part then softened, it was waiting to be seen and heard. Of course, it wanted a new and meaningful job.

I have seen the child part that needs to stay small. I survived the childhood pain of being unheard and unseen by simply shutting down my voice. If I didn't speak, being unheard and invisible was comfortable and understandable. I could survive the world when staying quiet and minimising emotional needs. Blaming myself for not being enough, for not being okay, somehow made the harsh and confusing world make more sense to me.

These days I still occasionally find myself going back into 'shutdown' when I feel like my needs are not being seen or met, or in triggering environments that bring my nervous system back to old survival states. I still occasionally see this part of myself, making me small and denying my needs to feel safe. This part of me feels safe as a victim, and tells me that it is better to be small and invisible than risk rejection in a relationship by asking for a need to be heard or met.

Parts of Ourselves

So, let's talk about these parts of our psyches from a slightly different lens. "Internal Family Systems" (IFS) is a therapeutic approach that describes and directs exploration into parts of our inner world, our inner family. Our inner family members all present us with different levels of wisdom and understanding, different roles, needs and expectations. The IFS lens can help us with processing insights gained from our psychedelic experiences.

Managers
Managers are a protective inner group that try to keep us organised and safe by running our day-to-day lives. A manager may end up pushing for perfectionism and even inflict harm in their pursuit of safety and control.

Exiles
Exiles are typically the injured or traumatised parts of ourselves. These parts tend to be exiled by managers. Exiles can become increasingly extreme, ultimately overriding the managers to become who we are.

Fire fighters
Fire fighters are another form of protection that 'put out the emotional fire at any cost,' sometimes doing more harm than good. They do the fire fighting in many ways, including unhealthy or unhelpful behaviour, such as alcohol, drug abuse and eating disorders.

After a psychedelic experience, we are likely to encounter a wide range of emotions, thoughts, and insights. IFS can provide a framework for exploring these experiences by identifying and understanding the different parts of ourselves that emerge during and after the journey. Integrating our psychedelic insights within the framework of IFS can help us access the *Self's* wisdom to process and understand challenging experiences.

We can learn self-leadership when using IFS as a tool. IFS emphasises the self as the core, compassionate, and wise centre of the psyche. This self can provide us with a stable and solid point of reference during what can be overwhelming experiences 'in the medicine'.

Intense experiences can lead to insights that challenge our usual perspectives. The IFS lens offers us tools for integrating these insights into daily life. Through dialogue and negotiation with various parts of ourselves, we can work toward a more harmonious understanding of our experiences. When unresolved traumas come up in ceremonies, an IFS lens, can create a safe space for any trauma-experiencing parts to heal. Integrating IFS principles with post-psychedelic insights can aid us in addressing and healing trauma-related triggers.

Our experiences with medicine might reveal inner conflicts or contradictions. Again an IFS lens can guide us in exploring these conflicts, facilitating a deeper understanding of our underlying motivations and emotions. After our deep dives with the plant teachers, emotions are heightened, and we might feel emotionally vulnerable. IFS can provide us with tools to manage these emotions, promote self-care, and foster better emotional regulation. IFS encourages us to take ownership of our inner experiences and engage with them in a self-compassionate and empowering manner.

Visualization Exercise

If this resonates, you can read these words onto a voice recorder on your phone and create your own-guided visualization. Find a comfy place to sit. Think of a part of yourself that reacts in a habitual pattern, a pattern you want to change. Take a moment to focus on a spot in front of you, focus hard for twenty seconds.

As you allow your eyes to start to feel tired, close them and visualise the number ten. Imagine the number ten fade as you open your eyes. Close your eyes again and imagine the number nine. See the number fade as you open your eyes. Repeat the process for number eight. Allow your mind to relax deeper and deeper. See the number eight fade as you open your eyes.

Close your eyes and imagine the number seven. See the seven fade out, as you open your eyes. As you close your eyes, imagine the number six, seeing the six fade, as you open your eyes. Closing your eyes imagine the number five and allow the heaviness of your eyes to take you deeper into focused relaxation. Let the critical mind go. As the number five fades, open your eyes.

Close your eyes and imagine the number four. As you allow the four to fade, open your eyes. Close the eyes to a three. Open as the three fades out. Close your eyes and picture a two, knowing that your mind is relaxing and expanding into the infinite. Open your eyes as that number two dissipates. Close your eyes and imagine a one. Keep the eyes closed. Watch the number one gently fade as the mind drops deeper and deeper into relaxation, the body into blissful comfort. With every inhale, drop deeper and deeper into comfort.

Now imagine a beautiful staircase, leading to a place of infinite possibility. Imagine walking down, and with each step the body relaxes more and more. With each step, there is more comfort, more clarity, more insight. As the body rests, the unconscious mind has a chance to be heard.

As you reach the bottom of the stairs, imagine a majestic looking door. It is open just an inch. Now, push that door open and imagine your wise advocates, sitting around a fire. Some people see their ancestors, different versions of themselves, and their 'spirit animals'. Whatever you see, hear or feel – trust your experience is right for you. Imagine your advocates inviting you to join the circle around the fire. Maybe you can hear the sound of the fire. Perhaps, you can even feel its warmth.

Imagine asking your advocates for some insights, such as around the positive intentions that any old patterns or habits might have had for you. With an open heart, listen deeply, and feel, sense, see, or hear 'the why', the reason, the purpose. Many 'unwanted' patterns and parts of self were once the very things that saved us, brought us connection, or love. Perhaps you experience a wash of compassion for a part of yourself you resented, perhaps an 'ah-ha' moment.

Ask your inner advocates to present some alternatives to the unconscious mind, some alternative actions or attitudes that can serve your highest good. Tuning into all alternative actions and attitudes available now, as images, maybe sounds, symbols, colours or feelings. Give yourself time to learn all you need to in this moment. While you are here, by the fire, you may like to ask for any other insights, knowing that you can come back at any time, and insights will come to you from now on, even while you sleep.

In your own time, give thanks to your advocates, and return to the door. Walk up the beautiful staircase, each step bringing your body back online. With each step, more energy flows into your body, with each step, your mind becomes sharper and clearer. Finally with a 1, 2, 3, shake your hands, roll your shoulders and move your eyes around the room, focusing on different objects, back to this reality.

More on Child and Adult Selves

As we go through transformational periods of life, we tend to notice ways of being and reacting that kept us safe during childhood, and how these show up in modified ways in our adult lives. When something triggers your adult self (and similar thoughts, emotions, sensations or reactions show up, to those that manifested in childhood), do you notice childhood survival tools showing up too?

Perhaps the way your child part survived, comes back in a more adult form? How, and in what situations, do old tools show up for you now? Perhaps turning away from attachment, or sabotaging connections helped you survive the pain of not being held (physically or emotionally in childhood)?

If we experienced trauma or stressors in childhood, we might have needed to become very alert or vigilant to stay safe and survive. Hyper-alertness and vigilance around potential threats, or unpredictable situations might have spilt out into daily life, diverting attention away from tasks and scattering our minds. This highly changed state is very common and often served a purpose. It helped with survival, but recognising safety and developing tools to keep calm and focused is much more adaptive in our adult lives.

Similarly, less than ideal childhood experiences or environments can lead to impulsive behaviour as a coping mechanism. Children who have learned to act quickly to escape dangerous situations might struggle with impulse control. Traumatic experiences can also disrupt our ability to regulate our emotions, causing intense mood swings, difficulty managing emotions, or complete emotional shutdown. When, as adults, we can see impulsivity through this lens, with self compassion, we can find new motivation to get grounded, to take our time and really act from a place of clarity.

Perhaps hyperactivity was a way to keep moving, and avoid feelings associated with traumatic memories. Restlessness and fidgeting can stem from an underlying need to stay on guard and not remain still. The part that might have needed to be hyperactive was most probably adaptive or helpful, but perhaps now, that part can have a rest.

When we notice a charge in the nervous system, we can learn to breathe and ask ourselves if there is truly a threat. If not, we can give some thanks for the part looking out for us, but give it permission to stand down And maybe find a new more adaptive role.

If we have experienced trauma, we might avoid situations that trigger traumatic memories or emotions. This avoidance can easily result in us becoming withdrawn or disconnected. This is especially so if attempts to connect and be vulnerable as children, were met with aggression, or resulted in shame, guilt or blame. But avoiding and closing down does not allow for growth as adults. The part that is avoiding is doing its job well... But could it be time to give that part a new role?

Looking at Our Parts Writing Prompts

Sometimes medicine work will bring forward an opportunity to review and look at self-assigned 'bad' behaviours we may beat ourselves up for. Could these aspects of self, be the same parts of our psyche that *did their best* to help us navigate and survive difficult or even traumatic times in our formative years? What did you do, how did you behave, and what strategies did you employ to survive harsh childhood (events/ situations/ dynamics)?

The invitation in this section, is to take the time to observe, and explore the goodness or adaptive qualities around *how* the hurt child in us might have survived. Write down any initial thoughts.

_____

_____

_____

_____

_____

_____

_____

_____

_____

_____

Have any of the Internal Family Systems archetypes (managers, exiles or fire fighters) come into your awareness throughout your recent work? If so, what roles have those parts had in your life so far? Do they still help you manage aspects of your life?

_____

_____

_____

_____

_____

_____

Contemplating a part or yourself that you may have recently seen, what role does it play in your relationship with other people? Can you imagine, what positive intent it has had for you? How does it try to protect you? What is it trying to protect you from? Is it happy with its job? Would that part of yourself agree to try a new job or role?

_____

_____

_____

_____

_____

_____

What would your 'higher self', that part of you that sees all, and has a sense of unconditional love and acceptance, say to parts of you that might be suffering? What would the part that is suffering like to say back to your highest expression of self? What does he/she need?

_____

_____

_____

_____

_____

_____

Are there any other parts alive within you from your recent work? Perhaps you can sense a part of yourself that originates from a past life, or lives? Perhaps you can see a part of yourself that you have carried into your daily life from your ancestors or relatives?

If you had spirit guides or other energies visit you in your recent experiences, (very common when working with plant medicines), what insights might you imagine these guides would express to the parts of yourself you have judged as wrong or bad right now?

Self Compassion

Take this opportunity, (if it feels right to you), to sit and notice how it feels to focus your attention with compassion on an old behaviour/ belief/ pattern/ addiction/ way of being - that was at one point, a way you survived. Can you offer that behaviour/belief/ pattern/ addiction, a 'pat on the back' for trying to keep you safe, perhaps seeing how it successfully did so in the past?

What can you say to this part that wants to keep you safe when it shows up now? Perhaps, something like: 'Thank you for keeping me safe in the past, but I am now more empowered with new tools to cope.'

_____

_____

_____

_____

_____

_____

_____

_____

_____

Patterns Writing Prompts

Think of a current pattern you have maintained from childhood. By maintaining this behaviour/ pattern/ belief from your child self, what are you prevented from doing? Do you have ways of being in the world that feel 'limited', 'sticky' or outgrown? Who would you be without an outgrown behaviour, pattern or belief? How does maintaining the pattern, belief or behaviour serve you now? *(Some outgrown patterns give us reasons to 'stay small', to not to show up in certain ways, to avoid responsibility etc.)*

_____

_____

_____

_____

_____

_____

_____

_____

_____

- Who might you become without old patterns and ways of coping?

- Are there previously unconscious excuses that may now be conscious?

- Perhaps these stories about your limitations no longer work for you? Maybe they kept you comfortable and safe?

- When contemplating replacing an old pattern with a new way of 'showing up' for yourself and others, do emotions, stories in your mind, or sensations arise within you?

- Can you sense any anxiety or fear? Can you sense excitement or joy?

_____

_____

_____

_____

_____

_____

_____

_____

New Pattern Rehearsal

Shut your eyes and imagine counting from 10, down to 1. With each count, imagine the number in your minds eye and see it fade out. With each number, imagine waves of relaxation flowing through your body. With each number imagine deeper comfort and deeper relaxation. Say to yourself: 'I'm so relaxed, my body is deeply comfortable as my mind expands out.' Notice how your body responds to your suggestion.

Imagine, stepping into a beautiful, magical vortex, the vortex of transformation. By passing through to the other side of the magical vortex, you can easily allow yourself to step into the feeling of what it's like to be the 'new you' with your new empowering beliefs. Notice what it's like to embody your desired 'ways of being'. Notice how you speak, stand and move. See who you have become in relationships, work and in the community. 'Rehearse' this new you with all your senses, and the power of your imagination.

As you see yourself empowered, ask your unconscious mind to show you any insights around the next steps you can take in your daily life that move you towards becoming more and more empowered. When you are ready to come back into normal consciousness, suggest to yourself, *I'm coming back to my body, empowered, strong, focused and clear. I'm ready to get on with my day.* With a 1, 2 and 3 open your eyes. Shake your hands, roll your shoulders and move in ways that feel great. Rehearse this new you when you notice old patterns show up.

Levels of Compassion

Ordinary Compassion
This is when we are compassionate towards one another, express kindness, and live with an intent of general goodness.

Compassion of Understanding
This is the second level of compassion and is when we seek to understand what a behaviour is about, how it started, what is it doing, the cause of it, the beginnings of it, and what it's doing for you. What is the functionality of an addiction, pattern or belief?

The Compassion of Truth
This is when we want to reveal the truth or mirror the truth within ourselves and with the people that we are around, even if it's painful. We are not here to protect people from pain, but we are here to, in the

present moment, learn what is going on.

The Compassion of Recognition

This is where we recognize that there is something in another human that is also within us, seeing another struggling with what you are also working on, or have been working on in the past. The other person is like a mirror you can see yourself within.

The Compassion of Possibility

This is really seeing the positive possibilities that another person isn't seeing within themselves. Seeing and acknowledging who they *can be*, and what really wants to come alive within them.

Self Compassion

Self compassion is aiming to apply all of the above to oneself. And when these things are not feeling available, or are outside of our capacity, we refrain from beating ourselves up.

Compassion fatigue

This occurs when we may sense we are becoming apathetic and just can't seem to feel compassion anymore. This often happens when we are not giving ourselves the nurturing and compassion we are asking ourselves to give others. What are some of the things that you can do, when you sense compassion fatigue rising up within?

Forgiveness.

Life is for giving. Maybe life will always offer us opportunity for an on-going process of shedding and forgiving. Forgiving, in my opinion is one of the greatest gifts we can give ourselves. When we replay the stories that reinforce how wounded or wronged we have been and continue to experience all that comes with the constant mind movie, like anger, resentment and a whole array of possible uncomfortable emotional states, we just keep ourselves in a state of suffering. Whatever happened in the past, is back there. That person we might be resenting and breathing continuous life into, has probably forgotten the incident we are hanging onto. Holding onto a wound, just keeps that wound open.

Forgiving can be understood as letting go of the right to punish, judge and resent others. Forgiveness could be described as, actively intending to perceive misguided acts that have impacted us as having come from the other person or group's own suffering or unconscious, triggered state. If we can see our fundamental okayness in the present moment, the essence that is not damaged, we see there is no crime playing out in the present moment, so there is nothing left to forgive. Forgiveness unfolds when we become truly okay and whole inside.

The Essene Mirrors

The Essene people are said to have inhabited the settlement at Qumran, in the Judean Desert along the Dead Sea. They led a strictly communal life, had customs and observances such as collective ownership, electing a leader to attend to the interests of the group. They were forbidden from swearing oaths and from sacrificing animals. They are said to have been incredibly self-controlled, never allowing their tempers to flair and served as channels of peace, only carrying weapons for protection against robbers. The Essene people did not possess slaves but served each other. As a result of communal ownership they did not need to engage in trading. Other than their peculiar lifestyle, historians have

uncovered other interesting and still relevant teachings such as concept of the Seven Mirrors.

The First Mirror
The first mirror reflects to us that which we are. What we see in the first mirror is the image of what we are in the present moment. It is a reflection of our dominant state of being. What we send in the present moment to the people around us, is what we see coming back to us.

If we are surrounded by people who are dominated by anger of fear, we could benefit from dropping our own fear and re-focusing our thinking to find small things to appreciate, love, create, or care for. If we see joy and happiness around us, that tends to be what we emit to the world.

The Second Mirror
The second mirror reflects to us that which we judge. This mirror is something we have an emotional charge with. It could be something that has wounded us in the past and have not forgiven. If we judge and

condemn with an emotional charge, we will attract what we are judging into our lives. If you are surrounded by people whose behaviour causes frustration or triggers feelings of anger or bitterness, ask yourself, 'Are you showing me a part of myself in the present moment?' If you can honestly say no, there is a good chance that it is showing you what you might be judging at that moment.

The Third Mirror

The Third Mirror reflects back to us something we lost. When we see something we love and desire in another, it is often something we have lost, given away or had stolen from us in our own lives – consciously or more often, unconsciously. Every relationship we have, on some level, can be seen as a relationship with our self, given that we are the 'lens' through which all things we know are perceived. We often try to reclaim what was lost in finding it within another. We reclaim what we gave away, or had taken away as a child. It could be confidence, joy, innocence, honesty, integrity, courage, love etc. All of which can be reclaimed within the self. We can feel this mirror when for some unexplained reason we feel the need to spend more time with a certain person. Next time this happens, ask yourself, 'what does this person have that I have lost, abandoned, or had taken away from me?' The answer may be surprising.

The Fourth Mirror

The Fourth Mirror reflects back to us our most forgotten love. This could be a way of life, a loss or unfinished relationship. It could even be a past life where an undesirable conclusion was created. Challenges, life themes, pull-towards-causes, relationships, experiences, or careers will recreate themselves over and over again until we finally get it. This mirror also allows us to see ourselves in the presence of addiction or compulsion. Through addiction and compulsion, we give away, little by little, the things that are most important to us.

The most common addictions that come to mind are usually alcohol, nicotine, or other drugs. But there are also technological addictions, work addictions, or sexual addictions. Really we can be addicted to anything. The patterns unfold gradually over time, and gradually we can give away what is most important to us by giving our life energy to our addictions. We may recognize the pattern at any time and find our wholeness in healing rather than taking the addiction to its extreme.

The Fifth Mirror

The Fifth Mirror reflects back to us our father or mother dynamic. It is often said we partner with aspects of our father or mother. We can also 'become them,' acting out the same patterns we learned as a child. As children, our parents are like gods to us. The relationship we have with ourselves, others and the god/ higher power principle can carry the same notes as our parental relationships. A great question to ask ourselves is, 'What would I say to my parents if I only had one minute left?' and, 'What would I like to hear from my parents in the last minute of my life?'

Throughout life, we have the opportunity to heal our relationships with both our birth parents and our definition of God or a higher power by recognizing what the mirror is trying to show us. This mirror suggests that both the positive and negative attributes we give our birth parents mirror to us how we perceive our god or godess within.

There is a possibility that the words we use, (both positive and negative), to describe our parents have very little to do with our early caregivers, what we are often describing is a mirror. This is the mirror our parents have held up to us. The way we see our parents and the words we use to describe them can act as a mirror of our own expectations and relationships we have with our highest self, and our personal definition of a higher power.

The Sixth Mirror

The Sixth Mirror reflects back to us what is often referred to as the Dark Night of the Soul. This is the opportunity to meet our greatest challenges and our greatest fears. It is a chance to transcend, grow and harness the tools that we have gathered throughout our lives to confront them. We always get what we can handle and we have a choice in every experience to greet it as a powerful warrior, or a victim. Each difficulty shows us the possibility of overcoming and reaching higher levels of mastery. In this mirror, we can lose everything we have, becoming metaphorically naked before the 'dark night' and still find trust in life. We can act calmly and wisely, choosing to be non-reactive to things, so that we can learn from the experiences we are going through. It's exactly as Albert Einstein said: 'it is at the time of our greatest crisis that we can grow and learn the most.'

The Seventh Mirror

The Seventh Mirror reflects back to us our self-perception. Others will perceive and treat us according to how we perceive and treat ourselves. If we have a low self-esteem and do not acknowledge our wisdom and beauty, others will not acknowledge them. If we are angry, bitter and unkind to others, they in turn will often react in the same way. If we change our perception of ourselves, we change the world. All can be found from within. The only goal and point of reference in our life must come from within. It is the simplest, and perhaps the most difficult mirror to be believed. The seventh mystery of human relationships shows us that everything that happens in our lives is part of the divine order. If we can live with this in mind, we can better manage our feelings and expectations around various life events and challenges.

Triggers

What are triggers and why are they important? Triggers, to me, are our greatest gifts. When we feel triggered, we immediately know that we have work to do. We can instantly feel that we are carrying ammunition inside of us. When we don't react with blame and try to chastise the other for creating this discomfort, realising that another person hearing or observing the exact same thing would not sense our personal discomfort, we can take ownership. We can then move from a place of victimhood into a creator mode, where we are empowered, strong, and able to move forward with compassion for the hurt parts of ourselves. Taking responsibility for our emotional triggers, rather than blaming others, leads to personal growth.

We can learn and experience a great deal through practising a process of taking responsibility. By examining our emotional triggers, we gain insight into your own thoughts, feelings, and reactions. This self-awareness helps us to understand why certain situations, people, environments or words trigger strong emotions. Learning to take responsibility empowers us to manage our emotions more effectively. Instead of reacting impulsively, we can learn to respond, and respond after taking a breath, thoughtfully and calmly, thus reducing the intensity of emotional reactions.

Accepting some responsibility for our emotional triggers fosters personal development. We can identify areas where we may need to heal, grow, or develop resilience. This process tends to lead us towards increased self-confidence and self-esteem, where as blaming others often leads to conflicts and strained relationships. When we take responsibility for our personal triggers, we are more likely to engage in constructive conversations. We can express our feelings without assigning blame, which promotes understanding and empathy.

When we recognize our own triggers, we become more empathetic towards other people's triggers. We begin to understand that everyone has their own sensitivities and vulnerabilities, thus fostering a more compassionate outlook. Blaming others can make us feel like a victim of circumstance. Taking responsibility shifts the focus to our own emotional responses, making us feel more in control of our feelings and reactions.

Rather than focusing on assigning blame, we can learn to channel our energy into finding solutions. This proactive approach can lead to resolving conflicts more effectively and creating a positive environment. Blame and resentment can contribute to stress and anxiety. Taking responsibility helps us let go of negative emotions and contributes to our overall emotional well-being.

When we hold ourselves accountable for our triggers, we are less likely to engage in overly defensive behaviour. This paves the way for healthier, more harmonious relationships. To understand our triggers, we often need to reflect on our past experiences and patterns. This practice encourages mindfulness and self-reflection, which are essential for personal growth. Taking responsibility requires acknowledging vulnerabilities and areas where we might be emotionally sensitive. Embracing vulnerability can lead to deeper connections with others and a sense of authenticity. As we work through our triggers, we build emotional resilience. We learn to bounce back from challenging situations and become more adaptable to change.

Depending on the sensations we experience, we can learn where the ammunition from the trigger might be living, and where it may derive from. If we can 'relax into the trigger' and observe it, breathe and close our eyes, we may even see in our mind's eye a shape, image, entity, colour, symbol or other form that represents the trigger. We may see ourselves as the child who first felt this body sensation, fear, pain, a sense of not-enough-ness, etc. It can be helpful to imagine your adult-self comforting that hurt part, asking it what it needs now and acting on its behalf. Maybe, in letting go of some fear, self-doubt, or self-loathing, you can give permission to pamper yourself, be spontaneous and have some fun?

It's *not* normal to feel empowered and in control 24/7, nor is it normal to repress these feelings, or take them out on others. Taking our stuff out on others, is something we have all done, and this is not an invitation to beat yourself up, rather it's an invitation to reflect. Maybe in the past it was not possible to take responsibility. You might not have had the capacity, or awareness of your actions. But perhaps now, you can begin a practice of gently taking more and more responsibility, each day becoming more aware. We tend to learn the most from life when we can learn to lean in towards the lessons that uncomfortable feelings can bring us, sometimes triggering memories of being shamed or hurt in our earliest and most vulnerable years.

Triggers - Writing Prompts

Name three situations that triggered you in the last two weeks. What are the body sensations and emotional feelings that arose? How did you interpret what happened? What does this reveal about your underlying beliefs about yourself?

_____

_____

_____

_____

_____

_____

_____

_____

Use these short questions to explore your reactions:

- What emotion did I feel? (anger, rage, hatred, fear, sadness, shame)

- What was I (angry, sad, afraid etc) about? (i.e. loss of control)

- What did I make that mean? (i.e. that I'm powerless)

- When did I first experience ... (i.e. being powerless)?

- How did that make me feel when I perceived myself as ... (i.e. powerless)?

- Do you know that perception to be true and accurate in the present?

- Are you really (powerless) now?

_____

_____

_____

_____

_____

_____

_____

_____

_____

_____

_____

_____

Exercises To Change Triggers

Exercise one

Think of a triggering memory. When you are there, really feel it. Where are you, what are you seeing, who are you with? Where is the feeling in your body, what's it like? Now, stop everything. Shake or move your body. Shut your eyes and just imagine how you want to feel in this situation when you are completely non reactive towards it. Imagine yourself in two weeks time, when that thing no longer triggers you. (E.g. A sense of calm, confidence, empowerment, self-assurance, strong boundaries, compassion, clarity).

Imagine how you are when you are feeling how you *want* to feel. Really focus on that feeling you want. What is your posture like, and what are you feeling in your body? What sounds, and inner dialogue do you notice? What images, (or movie) are you seeing in your minds eye? Are you *in* it, seeing through your own eyes, or seeing yourself in it as an observer? Is it colour or black and white?

As you use your imagination to bring this new resourced state to life, notice how you feel. While you are in this good state, imagine what has triggered you again. Has anything changed?

_____

_____

_____

_____

_____

Exercise two

This one is an oldie but a goodie. Shut your eyes, feel that emotion, identify where it exists within your body. Imagine you can give the emotion or sensation a shape, a colour, or a symbol. What does it look like? It could be anything. It doesn't need to make sense. Whatever shape or form the emotion takes, you can then imagine pulling the symbol of the emotion or sensation out of the body and holding it in your hands. Take a moment to acknowledge it, outside of your body.

Then imagine or visualize it disappearing, vanishing in flames, or throwing it into the light. Immediately after seeing it leave, quickly re-focus on a positive memory (perhaps a place, person or even a pet that brings you joy, love, or a sense of calm). Imagine yourself embodying this positive emotional state. What do you see? Where are you? What is your posture like? Now Imagine that triggered memory again. Notice any changes in how you feel, what you see, or hear in that old memory.

Exercise three

Think back again to a triggering memory, something old, maybe from childhood. Now imagine, seeing that version of self on a black and white TV screen, down at your feet. As you see that 'you', down there, ask yourself, what tools did I need back then that I have now, that would have made this situation play out better? Maybe it's a sense of confidence, assertiveness or calm. Maybe it's a physical object (such as a hammer, a car, a magic carpet). Maybe it's an action (the ability to run). Really feel what it's like to have the tools you needed and imagine sending all the emotional resources that you have now, all the positive emotions and tools, down to that image of yourself when you were triggered in that old memory. Watch that movie of yourself down there, as you fully embody that resourced state.

If there is someone else in the scene, what tools do you have now, that might have helped them handle the situation in a helpful and healthy way? Can you imagine sending others in the scene what they need too? Watch as they also change state in your mind's eye. Maybe you sent them some compassion, some wisdom, or a sense of calm?

When you see that version of yourself, fully wearing the new emotions, and any others in the scene acting in healthy and helpful ways, and everyone has all the tools they need, imagine things playing out differently. When you are ready, you can imagine, bringing that old remembered triggered image of yourself into your heart, allowing that version to grow up inside you, fully merged and integrated.

Often, when we 'come back' after these kinds of exercises, we will sense less charge in the nervous system. The conscious mind knows that this is just imagination, but the unconscious mind codes experiences differently. The unconscious mind rules our reactions, and has a huge impact on the nervous system. It doesn't know the difference between a real or imagined threat or memory. Every time you imagine a positive element within an old triggering memory, you are carving out new neural pathways or 'choices' for the brain. If that old triggering memory can be re-experienced with an updated emotional program, when new triggers come into your world, your brain has more space to act, rather than re-act.

When you 'light up' the neural network of the trigger, use metaphor, create 'movement' (briefly change state) then light up the neural network associated with a desired state, like 'love', then immediately fire up the trigger network once again you start to 'write new code'. In this way we carve out new neural pathways, teaching the brain to re-act differently. Your brain now rehearses the trigger, then positive state rather than the trigger, then unwanted reaction.

Moving Stuck Energy

In the 'wild' we would naturally, unconsciously use physical action to re-set the nervous system after scary events. Almost like a zebra will shake, maybe have a roll, breathe heavily, snort and carry out other 'automatic' patterns, following a successful escape from a predator. This acts as a bit of a system reset, and the Zebra will not have PTSD. She will continue about her day, like nothing just happened.

Humans, being so 'domesticated', with many social rules seem to have blocked out and 'forgotten' how to complete these important cycles of the nervous system. Consider the way we 'restrain' people at the scene of an event, trying to control the victim's emotional and physical responses. Sometimes this is of course for preventing further injury, but often it is misplaced. This energy needs to move, and often

times, our rules keep this energy trapped.

Now, I'm going to invite you to move a little, if that's appropriate for where you are, and if that's something you want to explore. You might want to find a space where you feel comfortable to move your body a little bit.

Close your eyes and imagine an event that might have surfaced during your medicine work, really feel into your nervous system, sensing any areas of the body that are holding a heat or charge. Really open up and get super curious.

Maybe you can imagine seeing your present self, talking to your past self immediately after that event, saying, 'I wonder, if you could move in anyway right now, what physical actions do you need to make, (do you need to punch a pillow, kick something, run, jump, shake), what do you need to say (or yell), where do you need to go and what do you *really* need?' Imagine yourself clearly following through with what you really needed at the time. The great thing is, your physiology and biology actually changes with your imagination.

As your body revisits this incident, be gentle with yourself. After the visualisation, you might want to notice any subtle sensations, any energy moving into parts of your body that want to move, shake, twist, turn, jump... release... If it feels right to you, you could choose to get up and allow that energy to flow. Notice any remaining sense of constriction in your body, light it up with your mind, really intensify and exaggerate the sensation.

Then, knowing you can choose to shift it with your mind and focus (*If you can 'turn it up, you can turn it down'*). Close your eyes and let it go with a number of deep breaths. Be open to the possibility that you can easily use your powerful imagination to see a visual representation of tension leaving your body. Maybe you want to see a beautiful waterfall in your mind's eye, falling from the top of your head, clearing out all tension as it flows to the tips of your toes, taking all pain, all tension into the earth where it can be transformed back into pure energy. Maybe you see a light flooding your body, taking all the tension away, maybe you don't see anything, and you just want to imagine feeling a warm breeze flowing through all your cells, releasing the tension from your body. Perhaps it's possible, to imagine a swirling tension or anxiety rising from where it normally spins around – and to give it an exit point, maybe squeezing the fists, seeing that energy travelling up the body, down the arms, and into the hands, seeing it flow out as you relax those fists.

You might like to create a mantra in your mind as you focus your attention: 'I easily feel into my body, appreciating each cell, just relaxing deeply with each inhale. With each exhale, all tension leaves, and healing flows in.' Is there a physical practice that you feel drawn to that can help you move into your body to charge and discharge as needed? (tai chi, chi gong, yoga, hiking in nature etc).

Nervous System Regulation Shifting into the Peripheral to Break an Anxiety State

Find a point in front of you to focus your vision upon. Focus on the fine details of that point. This accentuates the 'tunnel vision' stress response for a few moments. When you know you are really focused, without moving your head or eyes, shift your gaze out. Without moving your eyes, notice what exists on either side of that point of focus. What is above and below? Notice the objects, the way the light is falling, the shapes and colours, all the while keeping your eyes and head, totally still. Become aware of all that space around you, even behind you. You also might notice your breathing becoming deeper and deeper. Notice stillness. Notice the space between spaces, the silence between sounds. Now ask yourself: 'What is everything I'm not currently noticing, that is *not* making me anxious?' From here you can begin to focus your attention upon all the things that are okay.

Bilateral Stimulation

Bilateral stimulation engages both hemispheres of the brain simultaneously. It can be helpful in integrating thoughts and emotions, facilitating the processing of distressing or traumatic memories. This, in turn, can lead to a reduction in anxiety as the brain becomes more balanced. Bilateral stimulation tends to be rhythmic, repetitive and diverts our attention away from distressing thoughts. It interrupts the anxiety cycle and brings about a sense of calm. Bilateral stimulation can trigger the parasympathetic nervous system, which is responsible for the body's 'rest and digest' response, counteracting the fight-or-flight response that comes along with anxiety and distress. Bilateral stimulation can enhance the brain's ability to rewire itself, promoting new neural connections and weakening existing ones that maintain unwanted anxious thought patterns.

Left to Right Hand Pass

Start by holding an object at the centre line of the body in your right hand. Watch as your left-hand travels to meet the right hand holding the object in the centre. Watch as you pass the object from your right hand in the centre, to the left hand. Watch as your left hand carries the object to the left side of the body. Watch as you pass the object back to meet the right hand waiting in the centre. Watch as your right hand moves the object to the right. Watch as your right hand travels back to centre, passing the object back to the left hand. Watch as the left hand carries the object back to the left. Watch as your left hand passes the object back to the right hand, waiting in the centre. Watch as your right hand carries the object to the right. Watch as your right hand travels with the object back to centre, and again passes the object to the left hand. Continue the cycle, activating both hemispheres of the brain.

More Bi-Lateral Stimulation Exercises

Bilateral Music or Sound: Listen to music or sounds through headphones where the audio alternates between the left and right channels. The shifting sound can have a calming and balancing effect on the brain.

Bilateral Breathing: Take slow, deep breaths, and as you exhale, alternate which nostril you breathe out of by closing one nostril with your finger and breathing out through the other. This balances the airflow and can be relaxing.

Bilateral Drawing: With a pen and paper, draw simple shapes or patterns using both hands simultaneously. This can help engage both hemispheres of the brain and promote relaxation.

Bilateral Hand Squeezes: Hold a soft stress ball or similar object in both hands and squeeze it rhythmically. As you do this, focus on your anxiety and imagine it being squeezed out of your body.

Bilateral Walk or March: Take a walk or march in place, paying attention to the rhythmic movement of your legs and the sensation in your feet as they hit the ground alternately.

Bilateral Self-Hug: Cross your arms over your chest and give yourself a hug, alternating which arm is on top. Focus on the feeling of your arms moving and the comforting sensation of hugging yourself.

Bilateral Swaying or Rocking: Stand up and gently sway or rock back and forth, transferring your weight from one foot to the other. This rhythmic motion can be very soothing.

Fast EFT

To perform EFT, begin by imagining a time or place where you experienced peace and tranquillity. What do you see? Who are you with? What are your feelings? Bring yourself to a state where you are there, sensing on all levels. Get a clear picture and feeling. As you deeply feel this experience of peace, take hold of your wrist with your hand, palm up, almost as if you are going to take your own pulse. You can give the side of the wrist bone a little squeeze. Really feel the sensation. As you take hold of your wrist, breath in, and as you exhale say *peace* to yourself. Repeat this breath and word, three times to anchor. Know that you are going to come back to this.

Identify the root: For this technique to be effective, you should first identify the root of the fear, anxiety, or other emotional state you are shifting. Simply close your eyes and 'try it on.' Really get into the emotional state you will be changing.

Test the initial intensity: Once you are 'in' you need to set a benchmark level of intensity. The intensity level is rated on a scale from 0 to 10, with 10 being the most intense. Knowing your benchmark helps you monitor your progress after performing a fast EFT sequence. Get comfortable with the change phrase: 'I release and let it go.'

Fast EFT tapping sequence: The fast EFT tapping sequence is the methodical tapping on the ends of four meridian points. This is kind of like self-administered acupuncture. Once again 'step into the state' you wish to change.

- Begin by tapping the area between your eyebrows, with your index and second finger, while simultaneously reciting the 'change phrase' *(I release and let it go)* three times.

- Next, tap the temple area, simultaneously reciting the 'change phrase' *(I release and let it go)* three times.

- Now tap the area below the eye, mid lower eye socket, simultaneously reciting the 'change phrase' *(I release and let it go)* three times.

- And now tap the area where your collarbones meet, the top of the sternum, while simultaneously reciting the 'change phrase', *(I release and let it go)* three times.

Repeat this sequence two or three times.

Anchoring: At the end of your last tapping cycle, breathe and take hold of your wrist with your hand, palm up, almost as if you are going to take your own pulse. You can give the side of the wrist bone a little squeeze, really feeling the sensation. Now bring to the mind and body that vivid scene of peace and tranquillity, saying to yourself *peace* as you notice perhaps, your breathing slow, and subtle changes in your emotional state.

Test the intensity: At the end of your sequence, rate your intensity level on a scale from 0 to 10. Compare your results with your initial intensity level. If you haven't reached 0, you can repeat this process until you do. There are videos on YouTube that can help you visualise the flow of this technique.

Havening

Once again, think and feel the state you wish to change in a triggering situation. Rate the intensity like you did during the Fast EFT exercise. Next, rub your hands together slowly as if you're washing your hands. Give yourself a hug. Place the palms of your hands on your opposite shoulders and rub them down your arms to your elbows. Now gently carry out the action of 'washing' your face in a soothing way. Place your fingertips up high on your forehead just within your hairline and then let your fingers fall down your face to your chin. Notice any changes in your emotional charge as you think back to the trigger.

Heart Math's Freeze-Frame Process

Heart Math is an amazing organisation and I recommend checking out their website for heaps of insightful material. This simple exercise of theirs can be done very quickly to combat stress, sadness, depression, or anxiety by developing great 'heart coherence.'

When you notice you are feeling stressed or anxious, begin by taking some time out (even a few minutes will do) to disengage from the thoughts that are causing you stress by doing the following:

- Focus on the physical area of your heart (heart, lungs, chest, and upper back areas).

- Imagine that you can breathe in and out through your heart, taking several deep, slow breaths.

- Think of a positive experience from the past, a time when you felt love for someone or loved by someone, a time when you were content, safe, cared for, etc. If you cannot remember a time, then you can make one up.

- Imagine, breathing 'through' the heart, even placing a hand on the heart. Let that feeling of love radiate through your heart and the rest of your body. Imagine "soaking your cells" in the experience.

- Spend a few breaths here, noticing any changes.

Growing your Tool Kit – Art Exercises for Closure and Preservation

Consolidating transformative and transcendental experiences can be helped by visually representing insights, teachings, abstract truths, and new life understandings using symbols, shapes, colours etc. With all exercises, notice image/object/shape size and placement on a page.

Notice colour and stroke strength/ width. Why small/large? Why a heavy hand? Why a soft/ non-committal hand? What would the shape/ image/ symbol say if it had a voice?

Stoking and Tending the Fire

Create a visual, symbolic representation of the experiences that have sparked a fire within you, perhaps new insights around personal, community, or even ancestral, issues or topics that light you up inside.

- What resources can you visually depict that stoke your inner fire?

- What do you wish to create, change or work on?

- What is fuel for your inner fire?

- How do you know when you are running low on fuel?

- Where will you get fuel from when you are running low?

- How will you feel as you become more able to sustain your fire?

- Why have you imagined your fire a certain size, shape or colour?

Encounters with Transcendence

Did you perceive metaphorical teachings? If so, how would you depict these (images, icons, symbols, shapes, lines, colours)? How would you verbalise the content or meaning of your image?

Obstacles and Tools

Perhaps various obstacles came into your awareness during your medicine work. If so, how would you depict these visually? Consider people, places, situations, your inner processes, challenges, addictions, patterns etc. What images, shapes, symbols, colours might represent your experience? Now consider any tools, strengths, insights and solutions that came to you during your experience. How can you visually represent yourself, using the tools in your image?

Self as the Lotus Flower Self as the Warrior

Sometimes when we do deep work, we experience aspects of ourselves as personal archetypes. The following is a fun exercise exploring our inner warrior and our gentle nurturing side that most of us have within.

- Take three sheets of paper

- Visually present a representation of your inner softness, your vulnerable side, your inner feminine.

- Visually present your inner fighter, your warrior self that fights for your purpose and what is right, your sacred masculine side.

- Visually present a combination of your abstract and grounded self, your connection with sky and earth, masculine and feminine. Nurturer and warrior.

- Consider how this divine combination shows up for yourself, for others and for the earth?

- What do the two parts need to share and express with each other?

- What images, symbols, shapes and colours want to come forward onto paper?

Safe Space Image

Recall a moment of peace, groundedness, safety, security or comfort from your experience

Drawing Out a Trigger

Shut your eyes and just imagine, a pattern or reaction you want to change, a trigger you don't need to carry anymore. Now feel what that trigger creates as a sensation in your body. Imagine you could assign this trigger, with a colour, a shape, an image or symbol. Notice what comes to mind.

Open your eyes and make a quick sketch on a bit of paper, representing that old trigger. Make this image small, and just draw it in grey. Put this image where you feel that trigger belongs, maybe left, right, maybe at the top, maybe the bottom of your page. Imagine, taking

the body sensation and transferring it to the paper.

Closing your eyes again, now imagine how you *want* to feel, how you will feel as this trigger loses power. Some people imagine confidence, empowerment, calm, or any number of states that feel good. Now 'try on' this new state. Imagine you can wear a cloak of this desired state. Feel it in your body. Where is it? If you could give it a colour, a shape, an image or a symbol, what would it be? Notice what comes to mind.

Open your eyes and make a large image on the same bit of paper, place this image where you imagine, this good feeling belongs. Make it large and draw in colour. Look at the large image and as you do, imagine other emotional states that you want to feel more in your life, especially in times when you are triggered. Imagine yourself full of resources, all your tools, all your strengths and talents. Imagine all the strengths and talents you are developing, imagine they are already with you. Allow yourself to add to your drawing, surrounding that small grey image with representations of all your positive feeling states.

When you are done, imagine the triggering moment again. Notice if the intensity has changed. Perhaps you are ready to make that grey image disappear? If so, you could consider rubbing out that trigger, and replace that image with one that represents an idea of wholeness, peace, or calm.

Movement and Breath

Doorway Push

Stand in the centre of a doorway, with your feet hip width apart. Bring your arms to your sides and press your left and right palms into the doorjamb, at about mid torso level. Push down into your feet and simultaneously outward into your hands. Take a few breaths as you push, lengthening the exhalation of each breath, even with a sound. Then slowly release your hands and bring them over your solar plexus. Notice your breathing. You might notice that it is slower and calmer, while your hands may feel warm and energized. Repeat the exercise.

Stand Up and Shake

One of the easiest ways that you can 'discharge' any anxious pent-up energy is to just shake yourself out. Stand with a strong stance on both feet, and begin to bend then straighten your knees so that you bounce up and down a bit without your feet leaving the ground. Once you start the movement, get your arms and hands involved. Add your voice if you want, allowing yourself to create any abstract sounds, or even words if speech arises naturally. Let it get to the point where the movement is happening by itself. Get in a flow. Shake until you feel your tension levels come down.

Woodchopper

The woodchopper starts with a wide stance, your feet planted about three feet apart. Ground really strongly into your legs and feet, clasping your hands together and raising them up over your head. Imagine you are holding an axe. Allow your back and belly to arch just slightly. Take a few breaths and let your energy build. When you feel somewhat 'charged up' and bursting with energy, take a breath in, then on the exhale, make a loud 'ha' sound as you swing your arms forward and down, just like you are hitting a chopping block with an axe. Then rise up again and repeat several times, allowing the whole body to move in one smooth release, and making sure your 'ha' sound is loud and proud! Feel free to practice with different sounds and words after mastering the 'ha.' When you feel like the energy has moved and tension gone, return to standing and pause. Notice what has changed for you.

Punch it out
Begin with the *stand up and shake* exercise as above. Next, imagine you are punching into the air in front of you. Make a fist in each hand, and alternate between your right and left fists, punching forward on the out-breath. If you have something soft to punch into, great, but otherwise the air will do. Using sound will increase your breath, which in turn builds up your charge.

Breath of Fire
This is a breath work exercise commonly used in Yoga. It is useful for when you need an extra spark and an energy perk. It lights the fire within and could be seen as a double espresso without the caffeine.

Sit comfortably with your spine straight. Imagine you are keeping a bit of string absolutely straight – from the top of your head, right down to where your tailbone tucks slightly as you sit. Place a hand over your solar plexus, between the tummy button and the breastbone. With your mouth closed, rapidly snap your diaphragm inward, as you force a quick burst of air out of your nose. Then relax your diaphragm and notice how the air comes back in by itself. That is one round.

This exercise repeatedly snaps the diaphragm in again and again, forcing the exhalation while allowing for a passive inhalation. Start slowly, and build up speed as you gain skill at this exercise and develop your belly muscles. A few rounds of 40–50 snaps of the diaphragm is a good place to start. Stop if you feel dizzy and simply breathe naturally.

The Winged Breath
This exercise, from the Sufi tradition often depicts a heart with wings, encouraging us to see and feel the expansive nature of the heart. You can think of your arms as the wings of the heart: they reach out, expand, and then contract. You inhale and expand your chest, opening your arms wide, spreading them like wings. As you exhale, round your chest and bring your hands inward, giving yourself a hug. Feel yourself embracing your own heart. As you inhale again, allow your chest to lift upward and expand forward, once again opening the arms out wide. Repeat several times, allowing your body to follow with any other movements or sounds that spontaneously arise. Then stop and notice if your charge has shifted in some way.

Twisting Breath
This is a super energizing breath that brings an increased charge into the heart area. Sit or stand in a comfortable upright position where you have a bit of space around you to move. Place your hands on your shoulders and hold your elbows out to the sides at shoulder height. Breathe in through the nose and twist your upper body to the right, allowing your head to follow the movement, looking over your right shoulder. Then quickly twist to the opposite side as you exhale through

the mouth, again allowing your head to follow the movement, looking over your left shoulder. Repeat 12 times, breathing in to the right, breathing out to the left. Then centre yourself, and switch to breathing in on the left and out on the right, as you repeat 12 times again. When you stop, take a moment to be still and feel the charge that the breath brings into your upper body. Make note of any feelings that arise.

Alternate Nostril Breathing

This exercise is a basic yoga breathing practice (pranayama) to balance the breath, calm the mind, and soothe the nervous system. It is excellent for balancing the left and right hemispheres of your brain, creating peace and equilibrium.

Sit comfortably cross-legged or in a chair, with your spine straight. If you are on a chair, make sure your legs are uncrossed so that your hips are level and that your feet are on the floor. With your right hand, fold the second and third fingers into your palm, extending your thumb and ring fingers. Take a deep breath. With your right thumb, close off the right nostril and exhale fully through the left nostril. When the breath is empty, breathe in once again through the left nostril.

When the breath is full, use your ring finger to close off the left nostril, and exhale through the right. Inhale again through the right, and when the breath is full, use your thumb to close the right nostril again, breathing out and then in through the left. Always switch nostrils at the top of the breath, meaning when the breath is full. Breathe out and then in again through the same nostril. Breathe slowly and deeply. Practice 10–20 rounds of this breathing, and then sit quietly in meditation for a few moments, or longer, caring for your body

Being the Medicine

Plant medicine (and other transformational group practices) inspires a sense of unity, harmony, a sense of tribe, connection and safe vulnerability. During retreats and deep experiences we often uncover empathy and compassion that we did not know how to access before. Then we hit 'normal life' and can face the challenges of the 'matrix' and a sense of isolation. It can feel like no one will understand, no one will get it. So, it can be useful to remember, they don't *have to* get it to see it. As you integrate and weave your realisations into meaningful changes across the fabric of your life, people around you will feel the changes within you.

What did you learn about ways of being in the world that will let you lead by example? Radical honesty, setting boundaries, saying no with love, being open, being compassionate, taking new perspectives? What personal and professional relationships can you *be* the medicine within? How did gifts show up within you and how can you extend those gifts outwards, how can you *be* the medicine that has helped you?

As you uncover deep inner truths and your worldview changes, remember to go easy on yourself. You don't need to process everything all at once. You don't need to act upon all your insights and make all the changes tomorrow. Consider the next smallest step, and it could be teeny tiny. Breathe, relax, allow and trust. Remember that suffering is an unquestioned mind. Stay with the spirit of curiosity, keep finding the possibility that exists, within uncertainty. Keep trusting yourself, the self that observes that there is an 'I' observing it all.

Thank you for your interest in working with plant medicines. I do believe that our collective interest in engaging with these teacher plants is divine timing. Perhaps 'the plants know' that we need their healing around the planet right now. Perhaps they know, we are ready to change and to heal ourselves so we may also work in synergy with all of nature.

You got this.

You are not alone.

Recipes

Here are some ideas that you can play around with if you are new to making food from scratch. I've added these sample recipes to help with general wellbeing goals, outside of the strict preparation window.. You can tweak some of the recipes listed, to meet ceremony diet guidelines - please follow specific advice from retreat leaders (in most cases salt, oils and spices will need to be eliminated in the preparation window) (*) Add, or omit, as per your personal preferences, your specific body physiology and guidance from retreat leaders you are working with.

 ## Tahini dressing

Juice of 2 lemons
¾ cup tahini
1 tbsp honey
2 cups boiling water
*1 tsp salt
*1 clove grated/crushed garlic
*Add chopped Italian parsley or
other fresh herbs if you want to
experiment

Method:

Whisk all ingredients together (add herbs after whisking)

Red pepper sauce

One jar of oil free roasted red peppers

2 tbsp tahini

2 tbsp almond flour or 1 tbsp almond butter

1 tbsp honey

*Optional ⅛ tsp ground cumin and coriander

*Optional dash of liquid smoke, mild smoked paprika, mild BBQ seasoning or *smoked salt

*1 tbsp balsamic/ apple cider vinegar or lemon juice

*1 clove grated/crushed garlic

*1 tsp salt

Method:

Blend with a stick blender

Miso tahini and ginger dressing

1/3 cup tahini

1 large Tbsp freshly peeled grated ginger (or very finely minced)

1 heaped tsp yellow or white miso paste

1 tbsp coconut aminos (plus more to taste)

1 tsp toasted or untoasted sesame oil (if oil-free, sub water — flavour will be affected)

2 tsp maple syrup or honey (plus more to taste)

2-3 tbsp water (plus more to taste)

*2 cloves finely minced garlic

*1 pinch sea salt

*1 Tbsp rice vinegar

Method:

Blend with whisk or stick blender

 ## Green goddess

1/4 cup tightly packed fresh parsley (loosely chopped before measuring)

1/4 cup loosely packed fresh basil leaves (loosely chopped before measuring)

3 tbsp loosely packed fresh chives (loosely chopped before measuring)

2 ½ tbsp lemon juice

1/2 cup raw cashews*

1/3 cup water (plus more as needed)

2 large cloves of garlic

1 tsp coconut aminos

1/2 tsp sea salt

1 pinch black pepper

1 tbsp olive oil

Method:

Soak cashews in very hot water for 15-20 minutes, then drain. This step is optional if you have a powerful blender or food processor (raw cashews blend

well in high-speed blenders). Add all ingredients to blender and blend on high for 1-2 minutes or until smooth and creamy. Taste and adjust flavour as needed, adding more salt to taste, lemon juice for acidity, or herbs for more herbal flavour. Coconut aminos enhance umami flavour / saltiness. If too thick, add slightly more water. If too thin or strong, add more cashews.

 ## Whole roasted cauliflower

1 x Cauliflower
1 batch of Tahini sauce (above)
1 tbsp Dukkah (mild) or crushed and dry fried walnuts, hazelnuts and sesame seeds
*salt to taste

Method:
1. Preheat oven to (180 C).

2. Fill a small baking pan halfway with water and set on the floor (bottom) of the oven. This will provide steam to help the cauliflower cook more evenly.

3. Trim the stem and leaves of the cauliflower.

4. Pre-steam the whole cauliflower in a large pot for 10 min to slightly tenderise (or 1 min in an instant pot/ pressure cooker)

5. Let the Cauliflower cool and then pat dry.

6. Prepare Tahini sauce.

7. Carefully flip your cauliflower upside down and pour on *most of* the sauce.

8. Let the sauce pour down the core, shake it around so it infuses the centre, and then flip the cauliflower over and use a brush to rub the leftover sauce (including any that seeped into the pan) all over the exterior for maximum flavour.

9. Place the cauliflower core-side down before baking and add a pinch of salt and dukah spice blend to the exterior for extra flavour.

10. Place skillet in the oven and roast for 35-50 minutes (depending on the size of cauliflower) or until a knife easily pierces the core. If you prefer softer cauliflower, then roast for longer. For cauliflower with a little bite, roast for less time.

11. To brown the exterior, increase heat to high grill and roast 2-4 more minutes, watching carefully as not to burn.

 ## Cauliflower soup

2 leeks, white and light green parts thinly sliced
1 head of cauliflower, cut into florets
2 cups (500 ml) vegetable stock
3 cloves garlic minced (if still using some
garlic) or fresh chives
¼ cup coconut milk
3 tbsp nutritional yeast
2 - 3 sprigs thyme
1-2 tbsp lemon juice (to taste)
Coconut oil for sauteing

Method:

1. In a pot, heat oil (if using) and saute the sliced leeks for a couple of minutes while stirring regularly. If not using oil, use a dry pan, adding regular splashes of water to brown and prevent sticking.

2. Add minced garlic, and cook for a minute or until it's fragrant.

3. Add cauliflower florets, vegetable stock, chopped thyme, salt (if using), nutritional yeast, coconut milk and pepper.

4. Bring to a boil, and simmer until the cauliflower is cooked and tender. Remove from heat, and using an immersion blender, blend the soup until smooth. If it's too thick, add more vegetable stock and blend.

 ## Pumpkin soup

1 medium pumpkin (2 1/2 cups pumpkin puree)

1 tbsp coconut oil (or sub water if oil-free)

1 leek (diced // 2 shallots yield ~1/4 cup or 40 g)

3 cloves garlic (if still using)

1 Tbsp fresh grated root ginger

2 cups vegetable broth (*DIY* or store-bought)

1 cup canned coconut milk (or sub other non-dairy milk with varied results)

2 tbsp maple syrup or agave nectar (or honey if not vegan)

1/4 tsp each sea salt, black pepper, (if using) cinnamon, nutmeg

Garlic kale sesame topping (optional)

1 cup roughly chopped kale

1 large clove garlic (minced)

2 Tbsp raw sesame seeds

1 Tbsp olive oil

1 pinch salt

Method:

1. Preheat oven to (180 C) and line a baking sheet with parchment paper.

2. Using a sharp knife, cut off the tops of the sugar pumpkins and then halve them. Use a sharp spoon to scrape out all of the seeds and strings (see notes for a link to roasting seeds).

3. Brush the flesh with oil and place face down on the baking sheet.

4. Bake for 45-50 minutes or until a fork easily pierces the skin.

5. Remove from the oven, let cool for 10 minutes, then peel away skin and set pumpkin aside.

6. In a large saucepan over medium heat add olive oil, chopped leek, ginger and garlic. Cook for 2-3 minutes, or until slightly browned and translucent. Turn down heat if cooking too quickly.

7. Add remaining ingredients, including the pumpkin, and bring to a simmer.

8. Transfer soup mixture to a blender or use an immersion blender to puree the soup. If using a blender, place a towel over the top of the lid before mixing to avoid any accidents. Pour mixture back into the pot.

9. Continue cooking over medium-low heat for 5-10 minutes and taste and adjust seasonings as needed. Serve as is or with Kale-Sesame topping.

For the Kale-Sesame topping:
In a small skillet over medium heat, dry toast sesame seeds for 2-3 minutes, stirring frequently until slightly golden brown. Be careful as they can burn quickly. Remove from pan and set aside. To the still hot pan, add olive oil and garlic and sauté until golden brown – about 2 minutes. Add kale and toss, then add a pinch of salt and cover to steam. Cook for another few minutes until the kale is wilted and then add sesame seeds back in. Toss to coat and set aside for topping soup.

Broccoli soup

1 cup carrot slices

2 heads of broccoli

*coconut oil

*½ cup red onion sliced (or
use a leek if not eating onion)

*1 clove garlic (if still eating garlic)

1 cup milk (almond or coconut, seed oil free)

2 cups vege stock

1 pinch nutmeg

1 Bay leaf

4 basil leaves

a few thyme sprigs

a few sage leaves

½ tsp ground coriander

½ tsp ground cumin

½ tsp ground turmeric

1 tsp black pepper (freshly ground)

* Pinch of salt

3 tbls nutritional yeast

1 tbls arrowroot (more for thickening if desired)

A few mint leaves for garnish

Method:

Slice the broccoli into small chunks, including some of the stems. Peel the carrot and dice into small pieces (about 1 cm square, though the size doesn't really matter, just that smaller pieces will tend to cook faster.)

Finely chop the mint leaves for garnish.

Mince/ finely chop the onion (if using)

Heat a small pan, add 1 tablespoon of coconut oil. Sauté the minced onion till soft, about 4 minutes, on low flame, stirring periodically.

Crush the garlic into the pan, stir and sauté for about 1 minute.

Add the stock, and the arrowroot, whisking it in to prevent lumps. Add the milk.

Keep on low heat, and simmer for 10 minutes, or till the liquid thickens, whisking from time to time, and checking that nothing sticks to the bottom of the pan. The mixture will reduce as it simmers.

Add the broccoli and carrots.

Add the spices, nutritional yeast and bay leaf.

Bring the soup to a quick boil and then let it simmer on low flame until the carrots and broccoli are tender.

switch off the stove and let the soup cool enough to be blended/ pureed, so you don't work with very hot liquid.

Once cool, remove the bay leaf and blend/ purée the soup, in batches if need be.
The broccoli and carrot do not need to be finely pureed, a few flecks or bits add to the appearance and texture of the soup.

Set the soup back on the stove, warm it and add chopped thyme, sage and basil.
Add a splash of lemon juice if you like a little sharpness/ splash of citrus

 ## Pizza

Base
2 cups gluten free flour mix *(find a great DIY mix on minimalistbaker. com)*
4 cups cauliflower rice (steamed and squeezed with a tea towel to remove as much water as possible)
1 x egg
1 x tablespoon chia seeds
1 x tablespoon psyllium husk

Topping ideas

Basil pesto

Italian herbs

Tomato paste

Nutritional yeast

Cashew cheese or natural cheese when you are outside of the
ceremony prep window

3 cups mixed vegetables (red pepper, red onion, broccoli,
mushrooms, tomatoes)

Method

Cauliflower rice - heat in a pot to just cooked, then squeeze it with a
tea towel to remove as much water as possible. You should end up with
clumps of cauliflower rice.

1. Add flour and Cauliflower rice to a large mixing bowl

2. Whisk egg in a separate bowl with the squeezed cauliflower

3. Add egg to the large bowl add psyllium and chi seeds

4. With clean hands, mix into two balls than should hold like 'normal'
   bread.

5. Roll into two thinish pizza bases

6. Pre cook bases in an oven (180 degrees) until just firming up but not
   fully cooked, remove from the oven and add toppings

7. Put pizzas back in the oven until toppings are cooked.

Mediterranean-Inspired Quiche with Sweet Potato Crust

crust

3 cups shredded sweet potatoes or standard potatoes

2 Tbsp olive oil or coconut oil

1/4 tsp each sea salt and black pepper

Vege filling

2 cups chopped bell pepper, cut into 1/2-inch squares

1/2 large red onion, halved and thinly sliced and other seasonal
veges of your choice

2 Tbsp olive oil

1/2 tsp dried oregano

1/4 tsp garlic powder (*optional*)

1/4 tsp each sea salt and black pepper

1 cup loosely packed chopped baby spinach

1/2 cup sliced kalamata olives (*optional*)

Egg custard

6 large eggs (organic, pasture-raised when possible)

2/3 cup plain unsweetened dairy-free milk (I recommend homemade
- or brands without fillers and processed seeds oils)

1/4 tsp each sea salt and black pepper

Method

Crust:

Preheat oven to 425 degrees F (about 220 C) and lightly spritz a standard
9-inch pie pan

Grate sweet potatoes or standard potatoes and measure out 3 cups. Then
transfer to a clean towel and firmly squeeze out excess moisture. Add to
pie dish, drizzle with olive oil, and sprinkle with salt and pepper. Toss
to coat, then use fingers to press into the pan and up the sides to form
an even layer.

Bake for 25-30 minutes or until lightly golden brown all over.
Some of the edges may get a little crisp — that's okay. Set aside.

Filling:

Chop the bell pepper and red onion and any other seasonal veges.
Add them to a baking sheet, drizzle with olive oil or add a spoonful of

coconut oil, and sprinkle with dried oregano, garlic powder (optional), and salt and pepper. Toss well to coat. Bake on a separate rack from the crust for 20 minutes, until soft and golden brown. Set aside. Lower oven heat to 350 degrees F (176 C).

Eggs:
To a medium mixing bowl, add eggs, dairy-free milk (seed oil free), and salt and pepper. Whisk well to combine. Stir in the chopped spinach and olives. Add the *slightly cooled* roasted bell peppers and onions and give it a good stir until everything is evenly distributed. Place the filling into the baked potato crust and bake for 35-40 minutes until the centre is set with a minor jiggle.

  ## Pesto baked Tofu

   1 (454 g) package super firm high protein tofu
   150 g vegan pesto (divided in two)
   15 ml avocado, or olive, oil
   1/4 tsp sea salt
   1/4 tsp garlic powder (optional)

Method
Preheat the oven to 425 F (218 C) and line a baking sheet with parchment paper.

Drain the tofu, then crumble it into pieces less than 1/2 inch in size and place them on the parchment-lined baking sheet. Add half of the pesto (1/3 cup, unless

adjusting the number of servings), along with the oil, salt, and garlic powder. Toss to evenly coat.

Bake for 20 minutes, flip with a spatula, and bake for another 10-15 minutes or until the tofu looks dry and golden with crispy edges.

Remove the tofu from the oven, let cool for a few minutes, then add the remaining pesto (1/3 cup, unless adjusting the number of servings) and toss to coat. Serve warm with pasta risotto, polenta, or ratatouille.

 ## Ratatouille

45 ml olive oil, divided or coconut oil

1 medium eggplant, diced into 1/2-inch cubes (1 eggplant yields 5 cups chopped)

2 medium zucchini, diced into 1/2-inch cubes (can use green or yellow; 2 zucchini yield 2 ½ cups chopped)

1 medium red bell pepper, diced into 1/2-inch cubes (1 bell pepper yields 2 cups chopped)

1 medium yellow or white onion, finely diced (1 onion yields 2 cups chopped)

4 large cloves garlic, minced (optional)

1 (783-g) can diced tomatoes

8 g chopped fresh basil (plus more for serving)

1/2 tsp dried oregano

3/4 tsp each sea salt and black pepper (plus more for seasoning eggplant)

1 tsp chopped fresh thyme (*optional*)

1/4 tsp red pepper flakes (*optional*

For serving optional
Polenta
Pasta (gluten-free as needed)
Crusty bread (gluten-free as needed)
Drizzle of olive oil

Method
Heat 2 Tbsp (30 ml adjust if altering number of servings) of olive oil in
a Dutch oven (or large rimmed skillet) over medium heat.

Once hot, add the eggplant and season with a
pinch each of salt and pepper. Cook, stirring
often, until the eggplant softens and begins to
brown — about 10 minutes. Transfer to a plate
and set aside.

Heat another 1 Tbsp (15 ml adjust if altering
number of servings) of oil in the same pan over
medium heat. Add the zucchini, bell pepper,
onion, and garlic. Cook until tender and slightly
browned — about 10 minutes.

Add the eggplant back in, along with the diced tomatoes, basil, oregano,
salt and pepper, thyme (optional), and red pepper flakes (also optional).
Bring to a boil, then reduce to simmer and cook for another 10 minutes
or until the liquid has slightly reduced and the vegetables are soft.
Taste and adjust as needed, adding more salt for overall flavour, basil
or oregano for more herb flavour, or red pepper flakes for heat. Serve
warm on its own or with pasta, polenta, pesto baked tofu, or crusty
bread. Optionally, garnish with fresh basil and a drizzle of olive oil.

Leek and Mushroom Chickpea Pancakes

Pancake

120 g chickpea flour

1/2 tsp sea salt, plus more to taste

360 ml warm water

Mushroom leek filling

15 ml olive oil, plus more for greasing pan

227 g sliced mushrooms (we used shiitake)

2 small leeks, sliced into 1/4-inch half moons

2 cloves garlic, minced

1 tsp dried thyme (or sub twice as much fresh)

9 g nutritional yeast

1 pinch each sea salt and black pepper

For serving optional

Fresh thyme

Sliced green onion

Method

1. In a medium mixing bowl, whisk together the chickpea flour, salt, and warm water until smooth. Ensure that the water is warm as it will help the batter thicken correctly. Set aside for 15 minutes.

2. Meanwhile, heat olive oil in a large skillet over medium heat. Add the mushrooms, leeks, and a pinch each of salt and pepper. Reduce the heat to low and cook, stirring often, until softened — about 10 minutes.

3. Add the garlic and thyme and cook for 1-2 more minutes. Turn off

the heat and stir in the nutritional yeast. Taste and adjust as needed, adding more salt to taste, black pepper for spice, or nutritional yeast for cheesiness. Set aside.

4. Heat a non-stick or cast iron skillet over medium heat (non-stick works best). Whisk the batter again to combine. It should be fairly loose. Pour 1/2 tsp of olive oil into the pan and rotate the pan to evenly spread the oil.

5. Scoop 1/3 cup (80 ml) of the batter into the skillet, quickly pick up and rotate the skillet to spread the batter into an even circle, then turn up the heat to medium-high and cook the pancake, undisturbed, until browned on the bottom and edges, about 2-3 minutes. flip and cook for 1 minute on the other side. Transfer finished pancake to a plate, turn the heat back down to medium, and repeat with the remaining batter.

6. Top the pancakes with the leek and mushroom filling and garnish with fresh thyme and nutritional yeast or green onion if desired.

 ## Kitchari

15 ml coconut or avocado oil (or sub coconut milk for oil-free)
2 tsp whole cumin seeds (or sub half as much ground cumin)
1 tsp whole mustard seeds (or sub half as much mustard powder)
22 g finely chopped fresh ginger
1 medium carrot, halved lengthwise, thinly sliced
100 g basmati white rice
150 g split yellow moong dal (or sub red lentils, but kitchari
        is typically made with mung beans)

1/2 tsp ground cardamom

1/2 tsp garam masala

1 tsp ground cumin

1 tsp ground turmeric (plus more to taste)

3/4 tsp sea salt (optional)

830 ml water

120 ml coconut milk (*optional* for creaminess, richness, sub more water if omitting)

15-30 ml coconut aminos (*optional* for depth of flavour)

For Serving optional

Cilantro (fresh coriander)

Lemon or lime juice

Steamed kale (or other steamed or roasted vegetables)

Roasted sweet potatoes

Method
Instant pot

1. In a 6-quart (or larger) Instant Pot, turn the *sauté* function to *low*. Once hot, add coconut or avocado oil. Press *cancel*, and then add cumin seeds and mustard seeds and stir until toasted and fragrant (the residual heat after pressing *cancel* will toast them without burning).

2. Add all remaining ingredients except coconut aminos. Stir to combine.

3. Put on the Instant Pot lid and turn to seal. Pressure cook on *high* for 4 minutes (it will take about 5-10 minutes for the Instant Pot to pressurize before cooking begins). Once the timer goes off, let the

steam release naturally for 10 minutes, then manually release any remaining pressure. If in a hurry, you can carefully quick release.

4. Optionally, add coconut aminos for depth of flavor and stir. Taste and adjust flavour as needed, adding more salt for overall flavour, coconut aminos for depth of flavour, cumin for smokiness, or garam masala for warming/clove flavour.

5. I like to garnish with fresh cilantro and lemon or lime juice and serve with steamed or roasted vegetables (sweet potato is a favourite!)

6. Best when fresh. Leftovers will keep in the fridge for 3-4 days or in the freezer for 1 month. Reheat on the stovetop, stirring frequently, until warmed (add more water or some vegetable broth as needed if dry).

Stovetop

1. Soak moong dal: add moong dal to a large mixing bowl and cover with water by at least 2 inches. It will expand as it soaks. Soak for 12-24 hours, then drain and set aside.

2. Heat a large rimmed skillet over medium heat. Once hot, add coconut or avocado oil (or coconut milk if oil-free) and whole cumin seeds and mustard seeds. Toast for ~30 seconds or until fragrant, being careful not to burn.

3. Add all remaining ingredients except coconut aminos. Stir to combine. Bring to a gentle boil, then reduce heat and simmer for 20-30 minutes or until moong dal is tender.

4. Optionally, add coconut aminos for depth of flavour and stir. Taste and adjust flavour as needed, adding more salt for saltiness, coconut

aminos for depth of flavour, cumin for smokiness, or garam masala for warming/clove flavour.

5. I like to garnish with fresh cilantro and lemon or lime juice and serve with steamed or roasted vegetables (sweet potato is a favorite!), naan, and homemade green curry paste.

6. Best when fresh. Leftovers will keep in the fridge for 3-4 days or in the freezer for 1 month. Reheat on the stovetop, stirring frequently, until warmed (add more water or some vegetable broth as needed if dry).

 ## Baked herby fish dish

680 g flaky white fish, skin removed
30 ml avocado or olive oil
3/4 tsp sea salt (optional)
1/4 tsp black pepper (a light dusting over both sides)
24 g fresh chopped herbs (we used fresh thyme, basil, oregano, and rosemary — go for whatever you have on hand)
30 ml lime juice

Veggies

15 ml avocado or olive oil
1/2 medium white, yellow, or red onion (optional)
2 medium tomatoes, stems + core removed, sliced into thin wedges
3 cloves garlic, minced
4 medium bell peppers, seeds + stems removed, thinly sliced lengthwise (I use green, yellow, orange, and red)

1/2 tsp sea salt (optional)

1 pinch black pepper

For serving *optional*

Lime wedges

Cilantro

Cauliflower Rice

Method:

Preheat oven to 375 degrees F (190C) and set out a 9×13 (or similarly sized) baking dish. Add fish to a shallow dish or plate, drizzle with oil, and sprinkle with salt, pepper, herbs, and lime juice. Toss to coat and set in the fridge to marinate.

Heat a large pot or Dutch oven over medium-high heat. Once hot, add oil, onion, tomatoes, garlic, and bell peppers. Season with salt and pepper and stir to coat.

Sauté, stirring frequently, for 8-10 minutes, occasionally covering to allow the peppers to soften. Stop when the peppers are tender but not yet mushy. Set aside.

Heat a large skillet (cast iron is best) over medium-high heat. Once hot, add fish. Cook for 2 minutes, then carefully flip and cook for 2 minutes more. You aren't looking for the fish to be completely done — just seared on the outside.

Transfer fish to your 9×13 (or similarly sized) baking dish. Top with sautéed peppers, tomatoes, and onion and spread the veggies to achieve an even layer.

Cover with foil and bake for 8-10 minutes, then remove foil and bake for 3-5 minutes more to allow the top to get slightly browned.

Remove from oven and enjoy. Delicious on its own, or served with Green Rice, Green Cauliflower Rice, cauliflower rice, brown rice, or white rice.

Staples

 ## Whole Buckwheat Bread

Cover 2 cups whole buckwheat with water and 1 tbls of apple cider vinegar

Leave for 24 hours then drain but do not rinse mix

Take half the mix and blend in a blender/ use stick blender

Re-combine the whole and blended buckwheat

Add ½ cup water and 1 tbsp apple cider vinegar and leave for another 12 hours

Soak ½ cup steel cut oats, millet or quinoa with ½ cup sunflower seeds and ½ cup chopped nuts (walnuts are the best). Add 1 tbsp of apple cider vinegar

Soak for 12 hours
Drain the mix of soaked seeds/nuts
with the buckwheat blend

Add 1 and a 1/2 tsp salt (if still consuming a little sodium), 1.5 tbsp psyllium husk and 1 tbsp

chia seeds or flax seeds - combine into a batter
*(Optional) add 2 tbsp goji berries/raisins and some spices such as mixed
spice/ cinnamon (sweet), or turmeric/ carraway for a savoury flavour

Bake for 40/45 min at 180 degrees

Treats

 ## Cacao Avo pudding

Ingredients
2 large avocado chilled
1/2 cup full fat coconut milk
1/3 cup raw cacao powder
1/3 cup maple syrup
2 tsp vanilla extract

Optional Toppings
Hazelnuts, almonds, walnuts or pecans toasted and roughly chopped
Coconut yogurt
Peanut butter
Tahani
Sea salt

Method:
Slice the avocados in half and remove the pit. Scoop out the flesh into a
food processor and add the remaining ingredients. Blend until smooth
and creamy, scraping down the sides as needed. Test and see if you'd like

to add any additional sweetener. Divide the chocolate avocado pudding between four serving bowls. Serve with your favourite toppings, such as hazelnuts and sea salt.

Smoothies

 ## Almond Milk, Coconut and Berry Smoothie

1/2 cup unsweetened almond milk

1 ¼ cup coconut water (unsweetened)

1 cup blueberries- pref frozen

2/3 cup raspberries-pref frozen

1 avocado

3 tbsp fresh coconut meat if you have some on hand

1/2 to 1 tsp super greens powder

Method:

Simple – blend it all up! Add more coconut water if the consistency is too thick.

 ## Pumpkin Pie Smoothie

1 cup steamed pumpkin or organic canned pumpkin

1 cup thick organic coconut milk

1/4 cup almond milk

1/2 avocado

Green Smoothie

1/2 avocado

6 pc cucumber

juice of 1/2 lemon

2 sm kale leaves

2 lg stems of fresh mint

1 sm firm pear or apple

1 cup unsweetened coconut water or filtered alkaline water

Another Green Smoothie

6 pieces of cucumber

3 medium kale leaves, torn

5 stems fresh mint

3 stems fresh parsley

1 piece fresh ginger

1 avocado

1 cup coconut water (unsweetened)

fresh juice of one lime

Blueberry and Avocado Smoothie
Note: This could also be used as a dessert.

1/2 cup unsweetened organic almond milk

2 tbsp chia seeds

1 cup frozen organic blueberries

1 organic avocado

2 tbsp more almond milk for blending

1 cup raw organic buckwheat groats, soaked w/ filtered water for 30-60 mins- rinse well and drain

juice of 1/2 an organic lime

1/2 tsp grated fresh organic ginger

Method:

Combine almond milk, chia and let stand for 5-10 mins until the milk thickens up. Place avocado and blueberries in a blender. Then add chia mixture and blend well. Add almond milk for consistency. Combine buckwheat with lime and ginger and spoon on top of pudding. Add some mint as a garnish if you like.

 ## Fruit and Quinoa Porridge

1 cup quinoa, rinsed

3 cups unsweetened almond milk

1 medium apple chopped small (save some for garnish)

1/2 cup raw walnuts, chopped

4 tbsp raw sunflower seeds

1 cup fresh organic blueberries

Method:

Add the quinoa and almond milk to a pan or pot and bring to the boil. Reduce to a low heat for 5 minutes. Add in the chopped apple, walnuts, seeds and fruit and mix it all up. Leave on the low heat until more liquid is boiled off or serve immediately for less firm consistency.

Millet, Raspberry and Mint Breakfast:

1 cup millet
2 cups filtered water
1 1/2 cup unsweetened almond milk
sunflower seeds
chopped walnuts
Raspberries
fresh mint

Method:
Place the millet and water in a saucepan and bring to boil. Reduce the heat to low, place a lid on the pan and simmer for 10-15 mins until the water is fully boiled off. Turn off the heat and let it sit for 10 mins. Add 1 cup of almond milk then turn heat back on for 1 min until the mixture becomes a little creamier. Spoon portions into open bowls and sprinkle with nuts, seeds, raspberries and chopped mint. Serve with almond milk.

Additional Support

For those who feel like some additional one on one support would be helpful, let's connect! I offer one on one support via video, phone and in person. Connect via my website to make an inquiry: www.bodymindtherapy.co

1 x one on one support session before retreat/ dieta
Personalised preparation support
How to set yourself up for success
Preparing family, friends and work spaces

3 x sessions (one per week) following retreat/ dieta

Support processing and making sense of any difficult visions,

lessons, or insights

Support with carrying valuable realisations into your daily life

Guided 'compassionate self inquiry'

Tools to process triggers, find your deepest truth and make lasting changes

Guidance around nervous system regulation

Integrative NLP

Notes

Sketches